FLOURISH!

A gentler way to grow people

Clare Nonhebel

Cover by Shirley Walker

"The world is dry and there are very few gardens"

Denis Ball

"We know that love and faith together create an environment for healing"

Faith Lees

With thanks to all the contributors

who generously agreed

to tell their stories

for this book

CONTENTS

FOREWORD: GETTING BACK TO THE GARDEN

I first came to Holton Lee in 2010 for a conference called Connect, set up in marquees by thirty local churches working together. People came for the day or camped on the field to enjoy a weekend of listening to talks, joining in the enthusiastic worship, chatting with friends and meeting strangers, picnicking on the grass together.

I loved the place and the atmosphere – somehow peaceful despite all the exuberant noise.

I thought the peace was due to the occasion – all that prayer! So I was surprised to find, when I next came to Holton Lee in 2014 for its Community Fair, that the same peace was still tangible there – and, once again, when the place was heaving with people.

Run as a charity, Holton Lee hosted programmes for people with all kinds of physical disabilities or mental health challenges, promoting activities to enhance health and encourage social interaction.

A tour round the gardens impressed me, from the welcoming staff and volunteers to the service-users who clearly took a pride in their work there. But it occurred to me, as I walked past neat rows of veg and then overgrown patches of ground and a weed-filled polytunnel, that as everyone was allowed to work happily at a pace they enjoyed, meanwhile the weeds were running ahead at their own pace.

The charity was asking for volunteers, but physical stamina is not my strong point and I didn't think there was much I could contribute. I didn't want to make a regular commitment then have to let people down. Except … over the next few weeks, I kept getting an image of that polytunnel. I could just offer to go in and weed it one day, when there was nobody about?

By that time, a good friend of mine was working for Holton Lee and she arranged for me to meet Emma Browning, project co-ordinator for the Flourish gardening-for-wellbeing project.

Emma explained that it was necessary to do DBS security checks on anyone using the site, as it was used by vulnerable people, so she put that in process. She agreed that I could go in at any time for an hour or so and the staff would open the toolshed and point me in the direction of the weediest and neediest patches at the time!

But just for the first time, she suggested, I could come on a Friday morning as the group was having a cup of tea before starting work, and say hello.

Coming up the long drive that first morning, I felt slightly apprehensive but the leafy environment was working its magic again; Holton Lee is truly a beautiful place.

Although it's just off a busy bypass, once you turn off the road it's like entering a different world, a 350-acre estate encompassing woodlands and heath and grazing land, reaching right to the untamed edges of Poole Harbour where deer often wander and myriad species of birds and woodland creatures live out their lives untroubled by the human visitors.

The community room, where the Friday workforce of service-users, Flourish staff and a few volunteers gathered before starting the morning's tasks, was a small space at the end of a wooden building divided into units originally designed as artists' studios and now used by various groups.

As I walked in, past a row of spare welly-boots kept for borrowing by anyone who had forgotten to bring their own, and entered the room, something happened to me. I can't really describe what it was, and even now it brings tears to my eyes, which may sound silly.

This was a disparate group of people, all ages, all ranges of health and abilities, but all looking up in welcome. Through the window behind them, looking out on to fields, light streamed through and encircled their heads. They appeared to be shining. And the thought occurred to me, 'There's something special about these people,' and then, more specifically, 'These people are special to God.'

For me, the rest is history. I didn't ever get to weed that particular polytunnel, which got done in the course of time, probably by the Monday or Wednesday groups. But for four years, every Friday – missing very few, which was really not consistent with my health record – a highlight of my week has been arriving at that hut and joining in with whatever the group is doing, whether digging and planting in hot sun, huddling in the greenhouse sowing seeds in torrential rain, or engaging in craft activities to make woodland-based products to raise much-needed funds.

Every week, it still feels like an unearned privilege to meet up with these fantastic people, none of whom could be described as ordinary. They are far more than that, and I hope this is something you may see as some of these extraordinary people share their stories.

It's all right for you …

but … if Holton Lee is such a 'special and spiritual' place, as many people describe it, how does that benefit anybody except the fortunate few who have the opportunity to live in that area of Dorset, on England's south coast, and fall under its remit?

I believe it's worth looking more closely at those elements that make Flourish work as a project, and make Holton Lee work as an environment for it.

With the growing awareness of the importance of mental health – and with increasing numbers of young people and even children falling prey to self-harm, mental illness and suicide – nobody wants to waste resources on projects that won't work or on fashionable theories that may prove harmful in the long run. It's worth paying attention to what works and why it is working, and see whether the key elements can be reproduced elsewhere too.

Let's start with a present-day story, from Holton Lee's current site manager, Steve ….

STORY 1 - STEVE

"I worked for many years in the licensed trade and became completely dependent on alcohol.

I didn't have the happiest of childhoods, a lot of bullying at school. I had one sister, 19 years older than me; she has three children, the oldest one a year older than me. At the age of 11, I had a breakdown and was removed from school, sent to a psychiatrist and put on Valium. At 12, I went to a special education centre, mainly for pupils who had issues with bullying and crowds, and was much happier there.

There was one fantastic teacher, Peter Shepherd. One day, 25 years later, when I was volunteering at Holton Lee, I saw a volunteer sitting having a coffee break – and it was him. He remembered me and named me – 25 years on!

When I left school at 16 I was already working in pubs at weekends and I started drinking heavily from that time on: it was the culture. Life was working in the day and drinking in the evening.

I became Head Steward at the Conservative club at 19, living in, and when the steward was sacked a year later for alcoholism, I took over the job. That was 1987. In 1989 I got married and in 1990 had a daughter.

In 1991, following in the footsteps of the previous steward, I was fired for being drunk on duty. Because it was a live-in job we lost the flat and were given a fortnight to move out. We moved in with my parents, for over two years. I started working in a Bingo hall, and continued drinking.

We split up when I met someone else and thought the grass would be greener. When I realised I couldn't drink if I was driving to visit my daughter, from the age of three there were only occasional visits, and birthday cards.

I married my second wife in 1999 and went back to working in the licensed trade as Head Steward at the British Legion. I got into a lot of debt, which I was hiding from my wife, and – again because of my drinking – we split up. It was meant to be a three-month separation till I admitted I had a problem, but I didn't: I thought everybody else had a problem with my drinking, but not me. My wife stayed in the flat and I moved back to Mum's.

Working at the Legion, I would have several beers at work then go home at night and drink alone. I had a couple of on/off relationships with people then in 2008 I was in a new relationship, but the drinking was an issue and we split.

I had a major accident at home. Mum had dementia and my sister was visiting daily so I was hiding the empties in the loft – standing on the bookcase to reach the loft hatch and throwing the bottles in. After one drinking session, I slipped and next morning was in a lot of pain so I phoned my nephew and got taken to hospital. I had broken my arm in three places and dislocated my shoulder.

I was in hospital for three weeks. While I was in there I was going out 'for a smoke', buying four cans of beer at a local garage and drinking them, still not admitting I had a problem.

With my arm in a sling for eight months, I wasn't able to resume my duties and eventually lost my job. My drinking escalated. My sister had supported her son through heroin addiction and he was in recovery, so she could see what was happening to me.

The only time I left the house was to get booze. To be able to get out of bed I had to have a beer can open ready to drink in the morning and I was getting through 16 cans and a bottle of vodka a day. I wasn't washing or dressing. I had given up on life - would go to sleep at night wishing I wouldn't wake up.

One day I decided just to give up drink, at least for a few hours. I woke up in hospital with my ex-wife and stepson standing over me; a neighbour had come in to see Mum and found me having a seizure and got me to hospital. I was resuscitated in the ambulance and my phone had somehow dialled my ex-wife's number and she heard the whole thing.

The doctor explained it was alcoholic fitting due to suddenly stopping drinking. So of course that became my excuse for going on drinking.

Eventually, in 2011, I reached rock bottom. For me, that was waking up every morning having to have a drink and then throwing it up, having trouble getting to the shop, avoiding looking at myself in the mirror, messing the bed and vomiting on the carpet.

My sister was still coming in, trying to talk sense into me. She was incredible. Finally it occurred to me that these people who thought I had a problem might be right and I made contact with my GP, who referred me to local addiction services, working on a gradual reduction of alcohol.

Then I went into a detox unit for a two-week programme and had group therapy and one-to-one sessions. At first it was my worst nightmare, to be in a room with people, but over the weeks it became easier, though I was still holding back from being really open with them.

After two weeks I thought I was cured and went back to drinking and sitting alone in my room, though I was still seeing my ex-wife and stepson, on and off, and they were supportive.

The turning point came when my stepson got married and I found out I was going to be a grandad. Two weeks after my grandson was born I went back into detox, with a big photo of him as a reminder of why I was doing it.

This time I really engaged with the sessions, with the local drug and alcohol services and with AA. After two sessions of rehab I went on the ADCAP drug and alcohol community after-care programme and in 2011 a group of about eight of us came to Holton Lee to do volunteering tasks around the site for East Holton Charity, as it was then – later renamed Holton Lee. Emma Browning was here, co-ordinating the volunteers.

I had always been fearful of anyone with a disability and used to shy away from the group that came to the British Legion when I was running it; I would get someone else to look after them.

But the first day, coming up the driveway, I felt a sense of peace and relaxation, coming away from the hustle-bustle and the thought processes that were going on in my mind at the time. Emma gathered everyone together and said, 'We are here to have fun, do some gardening and get people interacting.'

I don't know if it was to do with the environment – but it was just a little bit of rough ground with an old caravan that needed removing!

The initial group of seven or eight people was very mixed, ranging in age from 20s to 50s, with learning disabilities, Down's syndrome, and drug and alcohol recovery. In theory, it shouldn't have worked, but everyone gelled. One lady with a brain injury from a cycle accident had very little mobility but she was very good at coming up with designs for the plot.

ADCAP ran out of funding for the transport and supervision after six weeks but later, when Emma was setting up the Flourish project, she contacted ADCAP and three of us joined the group. For me, it wasn't so much about doing gardening as getting out of the house because I was still isolated. It was improving slightly but I was full of fear when I came here. After ten months, I relapsed for two weeks, around the anniversary of my dad's death, but by then I was coming to Holton Lee and I knew I couldn't continue drinking.

By the second or third week it was like family meeting up, sitting together for lunch and breaks and the group as a whole was welcoming to new people as they came in. It made a big difference to my general well-being: prior to that, I did go to the shop once a week with my sister, caring for my mum, but after the programme I could wander up to the shops on my own. I was still on anti-depressants but didn't need them as much.

We were on a six-month once-a-week programme and towards the end of the six months people were being prepared to move on to other placements. Some people were disappointed to be leaving and I was one of them. By then I had a real love and passion for the site and was really reaping benefits from being able to socialise with people.

Towards the end of the six months, I got asked to stay on as a volunteer, to help with the guys moving into the group. That was a tremendous relief and gave me a sense of self-belief: it showed me I actually had a value; I was not just a worthless drunk. And I could still be part of this group of incredible people coming there with all forms of disability.

Everyone relies on each other's strengths and makes allowances for their limits. We were building a pathway through the garden, which seemed to take an eternity. One guy with autism was strong as an ox and could do jobs that would have needed a fork-lift. We asked his carer if he could start digging out the soil around an old railway sleeper so we could all lift it out of the ground after lunch but after a short time of digging, he appeared carrying the sleeper over his shoulder!

I started volunteering two days a week, supporting people one-to-one, and was amazed by how quickly people were improving, not just their character coming out and smiles appearing on their faces, but even physically.

The lady who had had the bike accident was frustrated about all the things she couldn't do and got upset when she couldn't put the wheelbarrow away at the end of one day – but I pointed out that she had kept going all day, building a bank and planting trees with the group – much more than anyone thought she could have achieved! She moved away eventually but one day she came back to visit – on a two-wheel fold-up bike that she had ridden all the way from the bus-stop on the main road!

Eventually, I was offered the chance of working two or three days a week in the office, doing reception duties, checking people in and out of the holiday cottages and doing some of the tasks around the site. I was still doing one day a week volunteering in the garden, which was my first love – working with people and seeing them move upwards - but it was a real boost to my self-esteem that someone was prepared to employ me.

I will be seven years clean on 10 August 2019. There are still times when those thoughts drift in and then you have to use the tools you've been given to deal with them. And I'm still in touch with a lot of the guys from the recovery group: three live in the same block of flats as me. But there have been four deaths; not everyone made it. You can try to offer help but each person has to want to do it.

Flourish has changed my life completely. I have a great relationship with my ex-wife and grandson and I'm rebuilding the relationship with my daughter, who is 28 now. We didn't see each other for 13 years but now we can meet up and spend some time together.

A lot of years are missing from my memory. But life is good. I am very appreciative of what I have got and of having these chances of hopefully helping other people. If anyone from the various groups is having a bad day we can meet up. It's never an easy journey. So if someone in alcohol recovery comes to Flourish, often a member of the local recovery team will ask me to talk to them.

One of the best and the worst things about recovery is getting feelings back. I felt self-hatred for what I had done to family and friends; I felt self-pity and resentment of people 'interfering' and trying to help. You can't change the past; it's about moving forward and helping others along the way.

In the drinking years, I didn't have any emotions. I probably only grieved for my dad five or six years after he died. But it's no good blocking out feelings: block-out leads to blackout!

By 2014 it was clear that Holton Lee would have to close if another organisation didn't come in to merge with us, and in 2015 Livability came on board. One day my line manager called me to come up to the office to see the CEO when my session in the garden finished, and I was dreading finishing because I thought it was all over – but I was offered the position of Deputy Site Manager, full-time.

The Site Manager left in 2016 and the Centre Manager offered me the chance of trying out the job; I'm now Interim Site Manager, because they're not sure what direction the centre is going, in the future.

Communication is important, and being open. Yesterday we had a full-on day and I said to the staff I was going to take 15 minutes out to walk around the Flourish garden. When I went up to London for a meeting, everyone I saw on the train and the Tube was connected to a phone, not communicating with each other at all. But here there is a kindness and generosity in the relationships among people in the groups and all around the site. You don't find that everywhere.

Holton Lee is a magical place. For me, the magic comes from the environment, from the spiritual feel in and around the place and also from seeing people come in on day one looking like a rabbit caught in the headlights, full of fear and dread, then forming relationships.

All of those factors count: if you took the same bunch of people from Flourish and put them together in a different situation, I don't think it would work the same way. It helps to have the openness of the site and the space for people who can't cope with being crowded, as well as the staff and independent volunteers to sit with somebody who needs time out.

I've got so much more out of being at Holton Lee than I have given. I lost Mum while I was here and was volunteering the day before the funeral and the day after; it's a safe haven and there is a bond of trust.

It's not just about well-being but about making the emotional adjustment of moving on and helping others move on. These are people that anyone on the street would write off and see as incapable of making a contribution to society – people with mental health issues, Down's Syndrome, alcoholics ...

A lot of people feel something special about this place, though for some who come for respite or holiday breaks it's the middle of nowhere, with no shop, clubhouse or wifi! It's not an escape from life but it is a sanctuary, a place where you can sit with your thoughts and process things.

I think because this began as such a spiritual and special place, some of that spirit still lives on. I sometimes get called out in the middle of the night for a fire alarm or the breakdown of a hoist in one of the cottages or a report of poachers, but even in the pitch dark there's still no fear. You're all right. You're here."

STORY 2 - ADAM

To get a clearer idea of how and why the Flourish project has such an impact on the lives of some very different people, let's hear from some young people facing challenges as they grew up, who were placed in projects that didn't quite work, and why the tide turned for them when they came to Flourish.

Meet Adam.

And then Lucy.

And Josh.

Adam comes across as confident, articulate and funny. He is sensitive to the needs of people around him and often goes out of his way to include someone who is hesitant about joining in an activity.

"I came to Flourish because it looked really good on the website, especially the surroundings – peaceful and relaxing.

I'm 28 now. I did four years at college, including some animal care, then I went to two care farms but I had a lot of stress there because I could see the animals weren't properly looked after.

I had done two years of horticulture at college but I didn't enjoy it much, but at Flourish I really like growing things and I've started buying raised beds and things to use in the garden at home. It was good to have some knowledge from the college course but I still have to ask a lot of questions – like kale, I didn't know what that was!

When I first came in, I thought, 'Are they going to like me here? Will I say something wrong?' But we have funny banter and I've come out of my shell. It's probably the best place I've ever been. It's done me so much good. When I started here, my mum noticed a difference in me immediately.

I was bullied a lot at school. I wore glasses and sometimes had a patch over one eye, for a lazy eye, and my front teeth stuck out, so I got called Goofy or Four-Eyes. I have dyspraxia which made me clumsy and I had trouble getting my words out. The speech therapist was Canadian and I didn't understand her accent so I had to keep asking what she said. And I have dyslexia but my teacher at school didn't believe in it.

When I was nine, I thought I was different from everybody else. I would bang my head on the wall and say, 'I'm stupid!' And I would gouge wood – luckily not myself, but it was still pretty hard for Mum. I was diagnosed at 18 with Asperger's (an autism spectrum disorder) and at 20 with ADHD (attention deficit hyperactivity disorder).

There's no bullying at Flourish and everyone helps each other out if they're stuck. That comes down from the staff: they get along with each other and with everyone. I am more confident now, coming here, than I have ever been. Hopefully, people like me: they seem to.

A lot of people judge those who come here and think they can't do this or that, but they can do it eventually; it just takes a bit longer to process. And even if someone can't talk, you can read their body language. If you can overcome the obstacles and do something for the first time, even sow a line of veg, or take the dog for a walk on your own, it's an accomplishment.

I like harvesting, particularly if it's something I grew. And I could do potting up plants for hours and not notice the time.

I'm happy here – though it would be good if we got more funding so we could develop it more and so that more people could come and experience Flourish. Especially more girls!"

STORY 3 - LUCY

Lucy is a pretty young woman with a gentle manner, who contributes to Flourish by her artistic skills and empathetic attitude towards others.

"I was at college doing life skills but it was only three days a week and I wanted to do something more. I was looking for somewhere I could talk to people more because I felt I wasn't doing that enough - I was afraid I wouldn't get the words out. I had found it quite hard at school.

There were different choices of places I could go but my family had been coming here already, to bring the dog for walks, so we looked up the website. Holton Lee is very peaceful and I felt very relaxed here.

So we came and were shown round the gardens and I really liked it. I had done a little bit of gardening at home and I was doing floristry at college, so I started coming here once a week.

It was a bit daunting, the first day. There was a mix of people and it was quite noisy! It was challenging talking to people I didn't know but I did enjoy the work I was doing: flower-arranging and making up veg boxes.

I didn't really notice a difference in myself, from coming here, but my parents and people at college have said they see a change in me. When I first started, they could see how nervous I was. I do still get nervous but I am doing it!

I'm hoping to do just two days at college and two days a week at Flourish. I'm 21 now and I'd like to carry on doing voluntary work, maybe something with animals eventually.

Everyone brings something to the project, and people have said I'm good at listening and that I'm a very kind person. I pick up what people are feeling, without them having to say it. And I like doing artistic things; I like bright colours and I do art at home as well. I love nature: anywhere in the countryside is nice but here there are lots of lovely people as well.

I have one sister six years older and I've always had good fun with my sister. I did find things very difficult when I was young, though. I struggled at school, right from the start, because I have autism, which was diagnosed when I was about three. Other children would ask why I had extra help at school and say it wasn't fair.

At school I enjoyed art and they said I was good at spelling. I've written stories at home, mostly adventure stories, and some poems. I left school at 17 and did an extra year in the sixth form; I was also doing a life skills course that they made up for me but that was hard because the school's understanding wasn't quite as good as at college, I think because they didn't know very much about people that had different problems.

At college it was better and I found doing more cooking was very useful, and I did get to talk to people more there as well. I think people are easier to get on with when they have had struggles themselves, even if not the same kind of thing. I can understand how they might be feeling.

An option I chose to do at college was floristry. I love plants and flowers and I choose what to grow at home. I brought in some sweet pea seeds to Flourish, one time.

I find it difficult to tell people how I am feeling but when I can do that, it does help. Sometimes when I have told somebody I'm worrying about something, they reassure me but I repeat myself and need constant reassurance; I find it hard to reassure myself. So I have sympathy for people if they find life difficult; I know what they mean."

STORY 4 - JOSH

Josh is an engaging and colourful character – reflected in his frequent changes of hair colour and his taste in music - described by some older service-users as 'torture'! He has natural leadership ability and during a den-building project he organised everyone into specific tasks, without anyone resenting it.

Like Adam and Lucy, Josh had a few experiences of work and education that were not entirely positive, before coming to Flourish.

"I started gardening by helping my dad from a young age, cutting bushes and using the shredder, and I was looking for work in gardening when I left school. In Year 11, I went every Thursday to a farm, learning to plant things.

My first work experience from school was at a DIY store but that wasn't really my cup of tea.

I went to the farm for about a year and I almost had a place there but the project closed down. It was a bit disappointing but on PVP (Pre-Vocational Training) I still did a bit of gardening and also bricklaying, IT, mechanics, woodwork, painting and decorating.

I like learning something new but I didn't enjoy the paperwork because I had to ask for help and I was always left behind. I got through the maths and English exams; I had extra time. My doctors didn't know if I had autism or dyslexia or something else – they couldn't work it out. I'm a one-off. A legend!

I was about three years on PVP but the last year was about getting a job – interviews, CV and work experience in a charity shop. I didn't enjoy that much but it was only about six months and I liked the people; I still go in to say hello to them.

What the doctors couldn't work out is that I'm not afraid of people, so that doesn't sound like autism. I don't know what condition the doctors thought I had, exactly. When I was born, they said I would never walk or talk. But don't ever let your condition stop you from doing anything! I'm close to my dad and he pushed me to do everything, and I proved the doctors wrong. It got to the end of college – I was 18 or 19 – and I needed places to volunteer. I'm in supported living and my carer said why not see if Upton country park has got any places? It was right near where I lived and I went to see these guys and they said start tomorrow, working with us in the garden! It was what I wanted to do.

I didn't know what the people there would be like: they were in their 60s and 70s and they were a bit set in their ways. They've got used to me now but they were a little bit rude to me at first. I didn't let it bother me and there was one young guy I got on well with, and the ladies.

I was doing one day a week there and one day on a project doing old people's gardens, but that closed. After six months at Upton I met Keith and we worked together well.

I wanted to do another day somewhere and in Spring 2014 I heard about Holton Lee but I didn't know where it was and transport was a problem. I thought it would be a little farmhouse with a few volunteers. I went with the key worker to have a look around – and there was Keith, by the fire-pit! I didn't know he worked there as well. That was good because I did feel a bit nervous about not knowing anyone, so I said to my key worker, 'I'll give it a go!' and after a few weeks we got transport arranged.

The first day, it was raining – but it was a good day. I felt there was something good here, like everybody got on. I bonded with one of the staff, who was the second youngest person there. I was unsure about an older lady on the staff but then she started teasing me and I was teasing her back.

At first I didn't speak up much because I was afraid to upset people but being here has given me confidence to say what I think. I don't come across as quiet or shy but deep inside I was a bit wary and cautious. But I've found it easy to make friends here. I've gained confidence and picked up a lot of skills as well.

Everybody's very welcoming. From that first day, there was a good impression. I've been here four years now. I was originally meant to be here six months but then I got an interview to be a volunteer because I'm good with people.

I like making paths, doing woodwork and doing site work with the men. I've helped build a fruit cage and made garden benches and planters. And when there are open days, I've been a tour guide for the garden and talked to people. Maybe next year I might get qualifications, a tractor licence, or even go back to college for a year.

I would say to anyone who is finding life a struggle: don't let anything stop you. We all have our lows and our downs but talk to someone, get it off your chest, leave it behind. Even if you're feeling down, there's a positive side that comes out of it.

People learn something here: how to look after the garden but also socialising and getting involved with other people. If anyone's thinking of coming here, I'd say, 'Get on with it; you'll be fine!'"

STORY 5 – BEING UNIQUE

The Flourish project goes against the social norm of dividing people into categories according to need or ability, instead aiming to form community from, for example, one person recovering from a breakdown, another with a brain injury and others with drug issues, Down's syndrome, stroke recovery, autism, post-traumatic stress disorder, alcoholism, attention deficit disorder, paralysis, dementia, homelessness, blindness or depression.

In fact, such a diverse community reflects reality. Life really does consist of people in all these circumstances. It's just that society tends to divide people into those who work for their own gain, those who work for others' benefit, and those who receive – not recognising that it's all one. We all do all of it. Differently.

So how can one project work for everybody, together?

The answer is: only by forgetting the categories. No one fits them exactly anyway. As Josh says, "I'm a one-off!"

Focusing on our common humanity doesn't mean pretending that everyone is the same. It means respecting all the differences, the gifts and the needs, equally.

The real question, in forming an inclusive project, may be, "How willing are you to see yourself in the person next to you?"

Several Flourish participants have said that when they first came to the project they took notice of the way that staff members treated someone with more severe difficulties than their own, and how participants treated each other.

If one person has a bad day and cries or shouts, or another becomes confused or unco-operative or loses their ability to do a task they were able to do yesterday – is that person still welcomed? Still understood, still part of the community?

It's essential for everyone to know this – because tomorrow that person could be me.

It takes courage and compassion to identify with someone whose challenges are different and to risk being seen by others as 'one of that lot' by people who still judge in categories.

I once interviewed a member of the L'Arche Community who had Down's syndrome. When I asked him why he lived in a community, he said, "Because I'm mentally handicapped." I asked him what that meant and he said, "It means that people call you names in the street and say horrible things about you in shops." While it was encouraging that he knew the problem was other people's cruelty, not his own identity, it highlighted society's tendency to categorise and dismiss people.

A friend of mine who works as a prison teacher is often asked by new inmates, "What are you in here for?" Because he wears ordinary clothes, it's natural for newcomers to assume that, as he's not in prison officer's uniform or prisoners' standard issue clothing, he must belong to the only other category they know and be a prisoner on remand or with privileges.

Our social benefits system also works by segregating people into categories. A person with a clearly diagnosed disability or injury that renders them unable to walk, carry weights or co-ordinate movement is not expected to do manual work on a building site or be left to starve when they can't.

But when someone's need for temporary or permanent support is less definable, it becomes much more complicated. Depression can be more physically debilitating than a broken leg; PTSD with its nightmares, flashbacks, panic attacks and mental blanks can disable the sufferer from performing effectively in a job – but these conditions may not meet the criteria for being supported or referred for appropriate help.

The person is normal but it is not the 'normal' demanded by society: to be totally self-sufficient, consistently functional and in control of every part of their life and psyche.

In forming real community among real human beings, the problem doesn't lie with any difference in abilities or backgrounds or incompatibility of mindsets, but with a world view that demands that people should be uniform – or considers them flawed if they are not.

Of course, boundaries need to be set, for the sake of everybody's safety - welcoming those who come to share but excluding the few who come with destructive purposes.

Holton Lee has had its share of thefts, poaching, vandalism and flytipping by outsiders, rendering security measures necessary, but so far no one has had to be excluded from Flourish except by their own choice.

If we want to grow real people and real community, we need to build a gentler, more accepting world. That's what we're all in here for, after all.

STORY 6: THE BACK STORY

Holton Lee, like so many charities, struggled with obtaining funding and in 2015 it became part of the disability charity Livability, which was itself the product of a 2007 merger of two charities, John Grooms Association for the Disabled and the Shaftesbury Society. Both of these had been set up by philanthropists in the Victorian era, who found certain aspects of the way society treated powerless people unacceptable and who wanted to make their Christian faith mean something in their communities.

As in other times of change in its history, there have been anxieties at about retaining the vision and ethos of Holton Lee, which has always been about environmental integrity and sustainability as much as about enhancing the lives of people with all kinds of disabilities. Would the spirit of Holton Lee survive the change of becoming part of an existing larger charity?

There are plenty of pockets of beautiful English countryside that soothe the soul, but so many people have commented on the special atmosphere at Holton Lee that it's worth looking into the story of how the place came to be.

It's an unusual story.

Local people often make reference to the couple who originally donated this site to be used for the benefit of people with disabilities, and mention the Christian community that this couple – Tom and Faith Lees - set up in the early 1970s, originally in their own home in a nearby village.

The Post Green Community grew rapidly from a handful of house-guests to over 120 committed members - single people, couples and families – creating a 'city of refuge' by opening their homes to people in need, welcoming strangers and addressing issues that were hardly acknowledged at that time, such as childhood abuse, addiction and eating disorders.

Community members shared and swapped houses, jobs and resources to suit the needs of a constant turnover of people who came to stay for a few weeks, months or years, receiving help to overcome some crisis in their lives. Hundreds more visitors attended the twice-yearly camps and other conferences, camping in the paddock at the back of Post Green House.

The mix of hospitality, pastoral care, prayer and shared family-style living seemed to work wonders. People reported improvements in their health surprisingly quickly, and either moved on with their lives or chose to become part of the Community.

When the camps outgrew the paddock of Post Green House and moved to the area of neglected farmland that was to become Holton Lee, some of the Community members moved there too, renovating the old buildings, coaxing flowers and vegetables to grow in the sparse soil, and drawing up plans for a wider project for people living with disabilities and for their carers.

But a new millennium, changing demands and ever-tighter health and safety regulations, along with the ongoing challenge of acquiring funding for the new project, eventually led to Community members going their separate ways.

But was this history still somehow embedded in the projects now thriving at Holton Lee – Flourish gardening, Woodland Wellbeing run by Dorset Forest Schools for people living with dementia, ceramics classes, RSPB-sponsored birdwatching hides, a newly built recovery unit for people with spinal injuries, the long-running stables with carriage driving for people with disabilities, and a multitude of workshops, day courses, activity groups and events for visitors?

Could that investment of a sacrificial lifestyle on the part of the Post Green Community account in some way for this tangible sense of peace and acceptance that so many strangers still comment on?

And if so, who were these Post Green people: were some of them still around and if so, what were their stories and would they be willing to share them?

In 2018 a team had just been appointed by Emma Browning to train Flourish service-users in interviewing and film-making, for the purposes of recording a Heritage Lottery-funded oral history of Holton Lee.

It seemed perfect timing for the Flourish community to meet up with its predecessors from Post Green and to share one another's stories. And the more we learned about Post Green, the more we began to recognise echoes of the same spirit living on at Holton Lee.

This excerpt from a newsletter gives a hint of it:

"Locally there is a very big gap in finding work for emotionally handicapped young people who have no immediate hope of regular employment, and also for people wanting to work again after a breakdown.

"They need unpressurised working conditions, preferably in a group, to help them integrate with other people again. We already know God's love and strength in these areas and we are looking to him for help in setting up the rehabilitation side of our life in an ordered and financially stable way."

It could have been published yesterday but in fact was written by Faith Lees in 1984 when the Community had been going for over ten years.

The Post Green Community has been variously described by visitors as 'ahead of its time,' 'more like real Christianity than any church we'd ever been to,' and by some of the bemused villagers, as 'a bit wild and wacky'!

It arose at a time when religious orders of nuns and monks were attracting few new applicants, with a few exceptions such as Mother Teresa's Missionaries of Charity in Calcutta, but 'lay communities' of ordinary non-ordained Christians were being tried. Perhaps the best-known was the L'Arche (The Ark) community set up by Canadian priest Jean Vanier, where people with different abilities lived together, sharing work and prayer and home-life.

More popular at that time were the 'hippy communes' with an agenda of escape from the rat race to live closer to nature and experience relationships without any formal constraints, but these were beginning to show signs of strain, with many becoming inward-looking, detached from society and reliant on drugs to achieve an illusion of peace.

One member of Post Green explained the difference: "The communes were offering free love. The Community offered love for free."

Post Green existed not for the satisfaction of its members but for outsiders – people in need. And those people who came, in their hundreds, all spoke of the efficacy of that unconditional love that helped them move on with their lives and break free from addictions, trauma and damaged emotions, and even from physical illness and disability. We'll hear some of their stories later.

The Community was not offering a professional programme of recovery, though many members undertook training in counselling, but a simple recipe of homeliness, acceptance, reassuring boundaries and love. Mother Teresa of Calcutta once said, "The world is dying for want of a little sweetness and kindness," and described loneliness as "the worst of all diseases."

It's hard to imagine, from the viewpoint of a later millennium, how counter-cultural Post Green was at the time. For a baronet and his lady wife to welcome into their home – and invite to ceremonial events traditionally reserved for the titled, influential or wealthy – a constant stream of people from other backgrounds and nationalities, with troubles of every kind and a range of disabilities, was to confront a whole spectrum of prejudice.

Simultaneously disowned as irresponsible bohemians by their peers and resented as 'posh' by the class- and money-conscious, when Sir Tom and Lady Faith Lees' faith in God became a living force in their lives, they were rejected as 'religious fanatics' not only by atheists but also by nominal Christians who mistrusted inspiration. The Post Green Community leaders also had to mediate between the natural reserve of local villagers and the sometimes unconventional behaviour of visitors with troubled histories. This situation became even more complex when Post Green merged with the Texas-based Community of Celebration in the early 1980s and the small Dorset village experienced an influx of Americans with their unfamiliar culture.

As Faith wrote in her book, 'Love Is Our Home': "This was what Tom and I had to face seriously. God was impressing on me that our life was going to change drastically; that we had to be willing to lose whatever reputation and standing we still had among family and friends."

The desire to fit in and be comfortable with a particular 'tribe' or circle of society is intrinsic to human life – even key to survival. Knowingly to choose to be an outsider, in order to relate to those who are outsiders not by choice but by being forced out of mainstream society, is a risk and a sacrifice.

Many of the present-day Flourish participants refer to the anguish of being seen as different or even worthless, exiled from the fast-flowing stream of life by disability, fear or simple reluctance to be part of the harshness of our normal society.

This theme of being apart, standing out, being the focus of all kinds of prejudice, and forfeiting ambition and advantages to stand with others who stand alone, is one that runs through from the early days of the Post Green Community to today's diverse workforce in the Flourish gardens.

So what made this young couple with four children, a heritage of social privilege and a full commitment of local responsibilities, embark on this remarkable and often misunderstood choice of lifestyle?

The starting point for Tom and Faith was a crisis – though later they would see it as a godsend – that arrived on their doorstep while the family was on holiday in an isolated windswept village on the far northwest coast of Scotland. As well as their own four children, the couple had several nieces and nephews staying with them, along with Faith's mother and a friend of her mother's.

In an incident that sounds like a scene from an old Gothic horror movie, late one stormy evening, above the whining noise of the gale, there was a loud banging on the door. Tom opened it to a dishevelled, crazy-eyed man with a dark scar running from the corner of his eye down over his cheekbone, who spoke with a foreign accent, asking for shelter for the night.

Tom went to consult with the other three adults in the house. Faith's mother's friend protested loudly that it was unthinkable to take the man in, with children in the house. So Tom returned to say no, and suggested the man try in the village – which at that time consisted of one hotel catering mainly for weather-nonchalant fishermen, a couple of houses, two shops and a petrol pump.

The man said he had already tried. And the couple knew there was nowhere else to stay for fifteen miles around, too far to travel on a night like this, even though Tom had noticed the man had a pushbike leaning against the wall.

After Tom closed the door, he and Faith were troubled by their decision and Tom decided to go after the man, so he got in the car immediately and drove after him, but although the man could not have got very far on a bike, there was no sign of him on any of the roads, and no trees or shrubs to hide him from view if he had wanted to take shelter.

Next day in the village, no one had seen or heard of him. It seemed he had only called at their house that night. Faith and Tom became uneasy, wondering if this was a test of their faith in God. How far were they prepared to live out their belief in welcoming the stranger – not just family and friends and people they chose to invite?

As Faith sums it up in her first book, 'Love Is Our Home': "Here was someone who had turned up uninvited and at an inappropriate time, a person in need, and we had sent him away. If it had been some sort of test we had not rated well. We vowed to each other then that we would never again lightly say no to anyone who came asking for hospitality. Whether he sent the man or not, God must have been listening when we made that vow ...."

STORY 7: CHRISTIAN

It's easy to dismiss other people's 'spooky' experiences or to try to over-explain them, though of course not so easy to dismiss your own. Everyone believes their own experience. Anyone who hasn't been part of that experience is using guesswork or over-imagination if they try to explain it away according to their own references.

Perhaps the whole purpose of incidents that defy rational explanation is to shift us out of our comfort zone of believing that we can control everything by our own understanding.

A former Flourish participant who experienced both the outsider's rejection and the turnaround effect of a personal inexplicable spiritual event on his life is Christian, a man in his forties. He tells his own story here:

"I'm using the name I was going to be given at birth. When I was born I nearly died and the hospital told my parents not to use the name they first chose but to keep it for the next child who would survive, so they gave me a different name.

I was diagnosed with Asperger's when I was 39. I'm 44 now. A psychologist told me that having Asperger's had probably protected me from some of the things I went through as a child but I don't know about that.

My first day at Flourish was September 1, 2017. I found out about it through People First Forum – an organisation for people with learning disabilities or autism.

A learning disability is different from a learning difficulty. A learning disability is an IQ under 75, which I don't have. A learning difficulty is dyslexia, dyspraxia and other conditions. Autism and Asperger's are neither, though they do have aspects of learning difficulties because we struggle with social communication, new situations and changes of routine.

I find social situations very tiring and draining, coping with other people, knowing what to talk about, trying to make small talk, and also understanding expressions which aren't meant literally, like, 'Keep your eyes peeled,' or, 'It's water under the bridge.'

It's a matter of learning to fit in by copying other people, which can be good or it can be bad if we're around the wrong sorts of people.

It's easy to be misunderstood. We can think we're helping people, when they might not appreciate it. A neighbour of mine had her washing out on the line and it started to rain and I had seen her go out so I went to take it in for her, but she came back as I was taking her underwear off the line and she got angry. I was trying to be kind but, even though I explained, she has never been the same with me since.

The main reason I started coming to Flourish was because of awful problems where I was living, which led to depression; I hated going home. When I came to Holton Lee, I forgot about the problems at home, and the feeling of well-being would last about three days afterwards.

Also, it put things into perspective because I saw and heard how other people were living, difficulties but also good things, and I saw that not everywhere was the same as where I lived. I had come to accept it as normal when anything bad happened to me – like one time, my former neighbour came to my door with a knife in his hand and I didn't report it to the police or anyone because I had come to expect that those kind of things happened to me.

When I came to Flourish it was a safe environment. Neighbours didn't know where I was and gardening gave me an interest. I used to grow vegetables as a child but I never liked eating them because they became like my friends! I grew a marrow once and my mum put it into the oven and I kicked off!

When I came here I felt immediately accepted. There were no expectations put on me. Each person is treated as a person rather than judged by their disabilities. I could see that, just by noticing how people were interacting with each other. Even if someone struggled with communication, they were always included, not left to sit on their own in the corner.

I didn't really have confidence issues because I do public speaking: I'm a Learning Disability Awareness Trainer, which is volunteer work. I train County police and Borough staff.

I'm also a co-chair for the Council, so I will chair meetings about learning disabilities, about housing, hate crime, abuse, social care and the tendering process: when different organisations put in a bid to supply services to the Council for people living with disabilities, we decide which would be the best value. Last week I went in nearly every day of the week, then it might not be needed for a month.

Flourish has enabled me to have somewhere to go where I can be myself. The rest of the time, it's like wearing a cloak but here I can take off the cloak, let my guard down, because nothing's going to hurt me. If something did, I'd let the staff know.

I find the social side easier here than in general society because we've all got a common interest, which is the Flourish project, so conversation isn't difficult because we talk about gardening.

My problem is that I open up to everybody. Even if they ask me how much money I've got I'll tell them, because I feel it's being truthful and honest, but people don't ask those questions at Flourish. I had a friend who asked if I trusted him and then asked me my pin number. I struggle to understand why people would tell lies or take advantage of me. It doesn't compute in my brain. I think that's to do with the autism.

Before I was diagnosed with Asperger's, I had been with a mental health team right from the age of seven, and they had said it was all sorts of things: depression, then emotionally unstable personality disorder, then one time, schizophrenia; another time it was anti-social behaviour disorder, and even narcolepsy, a sleep disorder – because when people on the autistic spectrum get overloaded they can get into a trance and switch off.

I wasn't diagnosed with ADHD (attention deficit hyperactivity disorder) until I was 30 but I'm now on medication, which works. It all affected my schooling. I didn't go to any school from the age of 11 to 13 – but a lot of that was because my family was dysfunctional. They didn't want me taken by Social Services so they kept moving me to live with other people they knew. I did go into care eventually, at the age of 12, on a Place of Safety Order, but still didn't go to school.

Even in care, my foster parents gave me a box of toys and in it was a Ouija board, though they knew I was a Christian. So it didn't seem like a place of safety!

I don't think much about those times now because it doesn't matter to me any more.

The biggest thing that helped with my recovery happened on July 15, 2004. I had been prescribed Dexedrine for narcolepsy and I don't know if this was an amphetamine-induced psychotic episode or whether it actually happened as I experienced it.

I had become agoraphobic, never went out except after dark when no one was around, and I had OCD (obsessive compulsive disorder), cleaning everywhere five times a day. If I sneezed I had to clean the whole room again, and I wouldn't let anyone in because they might contaminate the place.

On July 15, about 11 o'clock at night, I went out for a walk. I was thirsty and thought the only place to get water was from the tap in the cemetery at the local church. I walked around the back of the church and – this is going to sound bonkers, I know – there was this ball of blue light darting about all over the place, at sharp angles, making a high-pitched buzzing sound, then it stopped in front of me, about 20 metres away.

I was looking at it and didn't feel scared but I suddenly froze, my arms lifted up, my back arched and I couldn't move. Then I felt my whole body vibrating and the high-pitched buzzing got louder and then the light hit me and went right into me. I went flying backwards so I was lying on the floor and suddenly all the memories of abuse in my childhood came back to me. I even remembered being born. Then I did feel scared, but energised, and ran out of the cemetery.

From that point, I was no longer agoraphobic; the OCD had completely gone – and I had had both of those conditions for years. The next stage, I found, was to accept what had happened to me: the abuse. I had had counselling about the things I did remember but when this happened, everything came back.

The next thing I needed to do was let the people know that I had remembered what they had done. In some ways, I wanted to free them up, as well as myself, because they might always have been afraid that I might remember, and I also wanted to let them know that they were forgiven. I felt that the fact they knew I remembered was punishment enough for them.

I also had to put right everything I had done wrong. I wrote a list. Like, when I was 10 I had stolen some stickers from a girl at school and told her it wasn't me. I bought her some flowers and left them with a note outside her door.

I had stolen some batteries from B&Q when I was 12 so I went in and told them and paid for them. They didn't know what to do with the money: they couldn't put it in the till because it was so long ago.

Then I went to Woolworths because I had once stolen a chocolate bar but they said they were going to get the Security people, so I just put the money on the counter and left. But it all freed me up.

After the blue light experience my pupils were massive, which terrified my mum. It calmed down gradually but if I went near any electrical pylons they would get enlarged again.

Someone said it sounded like ball lightning. Other people said it must have been the drugs or else I imagined it. But whatever it was, it changed my perspective on life. For myself, I believe it was God's way for me.

After the experience, I felt one with everything, connected to everyone, and that everyone was connected to each other. People have got more in common than they realise.

And it seemed there was no separation between past, present and future but that everything happened at the same instant. After I came out of the cemetery I heard a sound like a choir singing, 'Holy, holy, holy, Lord God Almighty.' I could feel the presence of God.

That's what put me right. I have not had anything happen like that since. I did see an angel once, when I was four or five. When we had prunes for pudding I used to take the stones outside and plant them at the end of the garden. This one time – it was winter time so it was dark – a bright light caught my attention and I looked up and saw a Being hovering in the air, above the roof of the shed, like a human being but surrounded by light and made of light. It didn't have wings.

I wasn't scared. I was told I must have imagined it but if I had, it would have had wings because that's what I would have expected. I just looked up and saw it looking at me. It didn't feel unusual and I just carried on up the garden to plant the prune stones and when I came back it had gone. I went in and told my parents I had seen this angel and they just said, 'Oh!'

When I went back and told the family I remembered the abuse –
the worst one was my grandmother but she had died by then – my
dad didn't say anything and didn't deny anything. My mum
apologised for everything she had done. But my dad, later on, said
that every morning when he wakes up he remembers all the things
he ever did to me. But I told him he was forgiven.

After the blue light in the cemetery, I felt like my whole mind was
fragmented into a thousand pieces and I could examine my own
mind and work out how I thought. I drew a diagram of the
conscious mind and even genetic memory and deeper areas I
couldn't access.

When people think about things, they keep looping back and it
stops them from moving forward. But once I could work out all
the areas where I kept looping back, I was able to cut that bit out
and go through new experiences.

I had always gone to church. I was born again when I was 11 and I
still believe in God. My family called themselves Christian but
there were serious conflicts: violence and sexual abuse and occult
involvement, and my grandmother, dad and mum were alcoholics.
My dad drank three bottles of sherry a day till he died.

My grandmother was an international clairvoyant and that
conflicted with the Christian side. In itself it's a gift – clear seeing –
but the Church forbids it because it's the wrong use.

When I was a child I was taken for exorcisms because I used to
kick off. When I was finally diagnosed with Asperger's I felt angry
because the kicking off had been due to autism, not to anything
demonic. Also, the Church didn't seem to accept gay people.

The sexual abuse was done by women. My grandmother was the
worst. My mum had a horrible childhood. My grandmother used to
sexually abuse her son and she treated my mum very badly. Then
my mother abused me when I was young, and got involved in
inappropriate relationships.

Once I walked in on my step-grandfather abusing my cousin and I
told my aunt but she just said, 'Don't say anything; it'll only cause
trouble. We all know what he's like.'

The abuse usually happened when everyone was drunk, so nobody
stopped it. But at family get-togethers, it was all Happy Families –
everybody pretending.

I stay away now from most of them. Just because you've forgiven
someone it doesn't mean you have to let them into your life. That
can lead to everyone playing games; it's not healthy.

I used to think I was gay because I'd been put off women by what they had done, though I actually prefer women's company, as friends, but I later realised I had been born gay.

I believe that any relationship, no matter what it is, should be based on love, and that's why I haven't had a partner. Sex should be a way of two people expressing their love for each other, not just making themselves feel good.

People think they need somebody else, to be happy, but you have to be happy with yourself first.

At Flourish, people accept you for yourself. It's easy to be happy here."

STORY 8: FAMILIES IN COMMUNITY

The impact of any kind of spiritual experience on someone's life is to prompt a life-changing decision: whether to deny its validity, bury the memory and persist in following a familiar lifestyle as though the event had never happened, or whether to take the risk of changing direction.

Christian tackled the challenge courageously – forgiving the people who had hurt him, trying to make amends for things he had done wrong, and restoring his own integrity as a valuable human being. The challenge for Tom and Faith Lees, though different, was equally life-determining. Tom had already sacrificed his original career plans when his elder brother's death in the war made him, as the younger son, heir to the family's estate.

Having accepted this situation, with its raft of responsibilities, he had thrown himself heart and soul into working - for the estate with its properties, tenants and farms and for local official and voluntary organisations, in education, the law courts, youth work, foster care provision and the Church. He considered the possibility of being elected to head up the County Council and even becoming an MP.

His time was fully committed and his work was appreciated and useful. He had been brought up as a Christian and never really questioned it, and was generally seen as a good man. But in the society he lived in, religion, sex and money were the taboo subjects, never talked about and the purpose of them never questioned.

What if Tom really committed his life to doing whatever God asked of him? What if that led to giving up reputation and status among people of influence, and any career plans for public service, and instead opening his heart, his home and his life to a crowd of strangers whose needs and numbers might prove to be limitless?

And Faith, as she became more committed to God, how much would she need to sacrifice? As a child and young woman, she had always rebelled against being told what to do and had followed her own way. Now, running a home, bringing up four children and extending hospitality on a regular basis to friends, family and anybody with a need to stay somewhere peaceful for a few weeks, as well as being a JP, her energies seemed to be already fully engaged and usefully directed.

But over-commitment and trying to meet everyone's needs and expectations, without a clear focus or boundaries, was leading her towards a breakdown. As she sought help for herself and began to experience the real intimacy of a living relationship with God, she started to form a vision for a future with no guarantees of wealth or security but with an emerging identity for Post Green House as a place of refuge.

How would this impact her family priorities and her children's lives? That was something they could all only find out by following this unknown path, one step at a time.

As time went on, and more people from other parts of the country, and world, felt that same prompting to open their lives and share everything, not for their own companionship and comfort but for the benefit of needy and hurting strangers, many other families had to face a similar challenge.

Becoming involved in a community would mean risking the unknown. So how would this work out for parents living in a nuclear family with their own children?

It was natural to feel, as Faith's mother's friend felt that night in Scotland when the stranger came to the door, that it could be unsafe to let strangers into the home. And in many cases, it would be truly unwise. To err on the side of caution, to make sure that this was really a God-given invitation and not a reckless whim or an attempt at virtue-signalling to others, would be only responsible. So when, in the 1970s and '80s, parents of families felt inspired to come and be part of the Post Green Community – whether living-in or travelling in regularly from somewhere else - they inevitably wondered how their decision would affect their growing children. Here, we hear from parents of three families - Jenny who came year after year to the Bible camps with her family, Jodi and Howard who joined from an American community and adopted four children, and Viv, who with her two daughters first came to Post Green for refuge.

Jenny and her husband Frank were living in Bristol when they first heard about Post Green, through contact with the Fisherfolk, a travelling singing group connected with the Community of Celebration that grew out of a church in Houston, Texas, and settled in the Isle of Cumbrae in Scotland before eventually joining with the Post Green Community.

Jenny recalls: "It was the mid 1980s and we were going to a church in Bristol that 'ticked the boxes' but we felt that there had to be more to Christian life. Frank was helping to run a Methodist youth club, and the club attended one of the Fisherfolk drama workshops. Frank met Jodi, who was with the Fisherfolk, and bought a copy of a magazine that had various Post Green articles, including one about Graham Cyster, a mixed race South African at the time of Apartheid. The articles spoke to us!

We saw an advert for an annual Christian camp. At the time we had three children aged six, four and a baby, and no tent! I remember making the decision as I was washing up: 'Yes, we *will* go!'

We came to Holton Lee with our three children, drove up the drive and pitched our tent on the field. The children loved it and we came back year after year.

After a few years, we were invited to become members. It was such a lovely place and it was clear to us that prayer was undergirding it all.

Holton Lee has remained a special place over all the years, through all the changes, regardless of finances, different directors etc. It's clearly soaked in prayer, a 'thin place' *(a Celtic Christian term for places where heaven and earth seem very close or to have merged),* and that continues to this day.

Holton Lee gives a feeling that you're coming home. I'm pleased that Livability, a Christian charity, now have responsibility for Holton Lee. Other organisations wanted the space but would have made unwelcome changes such as closing it to the public."

For Jodi and Howard, their decision to join Post Green was linked with their desire to have a family.

Jodi explains, "There were two reasons we wanted to move to Post Green. One was that I had had a vision, from a time in childhood when I had serious illness and was bed-bound for two years and dreamed a lot about the future.

Part of it was about being involved in education, travelling with bands, working with people, and being a singer-songwriter – all things that happened through Fisherfolk and the Community of Celebration.

And part was a vision of having a house of refuge, with a husband and kids, for people who were emotionally disturbed and worn out. In 1978-9, Faith and Tom came to spend a year helping with the Community of Celebration on the island of Cumbrae, and Faith and I realised we shared this same vision.

Early on, after we moved to Post Green, Faith and I would walk around the perimeters of the barn and the fields at East Holton (the site that became Holton Lee) and pray for it to be used for that purpose.

The other reason we moved to Post Green was that I lost a baby and couldn't have any more and we wanted to adopt - if possible a family of children - and there wasn't even provision for fostering on the island."

By joining Post Green, Jodi and Howard, who married in Cumbrae in 1978, could continue to live in a Christian community and bring up their four adopted children in that supportive environment. "We adopted four children who had the same mum; they were aged four, five, six and seven at that time."

A challenge for anyone but as Howard explains, "Being part of a loving community meant that the children had other people, godparents, making them feel special," and sharing the responsibility. For instance, each child had an allocated adult they would sit with at worship services. Jodi, as a singer and songwriter, would often lead worship at Post Green and Howard, later ordained as a minister, would often preside - "and the children were lively!" so this extended family arrangement worked well. Howard had first encountered the Post Green Community by coming to the camps as a teenager.

"Then after I graduated in 1974 I got a newsletter asking for volunteers to help in the building project at East Holton, so I came for the summer to help with renovating the farmhouse so it could be used as a community household. We eventually lived in the farmhouse for ten years with our four children. We called the house Sparrows Nest, because it provided a roost for our four sparrows!"

Living in community meant sharing accommodation, whether in Faith and Tom's home or in estate-owned cottages in the village or in the former East Holton farmhouse at Holton Lee – later used as offices for Livability Holton Lee.

Income was also shared, which made for a different experience for families. Viv came to Post Green with her two daughters when her marriage was experiencing difficulties. She recalls the impact on them of this shared lifestyle, including living on a tight budget: "We lived in Post Green House for some years: there were 30 of us there. Before that we lived at the Lodge, where there were 12 or 13 people.

Our children were very happy in the Community. The summer camps were very special. We had someone staying with us from Finland and when she went back my elder daughter went with her for the summer.

When my daughter was at the local school, for one cookery lesson they were asked to bring in the ingredients for crumble for all the people who lived in their home, and she insisted it should be enough for everyone in the household: in her case, 25 people! We always invited the children's teachers to come and have a meal with us so they could see how we lived, because several thought we were quite strange, a hippy commune or something. And as a nurse, I went on school camps.

So the children fitted in all right. The only thing they didn't like about the Community was the food: we had a lot of soya, and no crisps or anything. But we had to change that after they went to a party and the hosts complained they ate all the crisps and party food!"

Adapting to this different lifestyle was not a one-off but involved adjusting to the constant changes within an ever-growing community with numbers of transitory visitors.

Viv recalls: "We joined in 1974 just before the Post Green Community joined up with the Community of Celebration, when our children were four and six.

There was something so special about Post Green and the farmhouse at Holton Lee – they were still renovating the farmhouse when we moved down. There was a wonderful, spiritual, inclusive atmosphere that you didn't always find in churches.

At one time there were 130 of us in 13 different households, some in Lytchett Minster (the village of which Post Green is a part), some in Lytchett Matravers and two in Upton. We met every evening for chapel time at St Dunstans church in Upton and had a shared meal all together once a week.

We had 50p pocket money a week and £6.25 per head to cover food, petrol, clothing, household goods, presents, everything. I remember the exact amount because it was so hard to make it stretch! We used to dilute the margarine with cooking oil to make it go farther. And we would buy food for a lot of households at once – we did a meat run and a veg run – not just for Community members: for people in the village as well.

We ran the caravan site and for a while I was the postmistress at Post Green village shop, and we ran the garage for a while, and ran the Fisherfolk record business from next door to the post office. Some Community members were teachers and one worked in a bank. All those incomes were pooled and so were the Family Allowances, and all the Community members' allowances were paid out of that.

Although people committed to be part of the Community for life, Tom Lees was careful to ensure that they could change their minds, so if they put everything into the Community and wanted to leave they weren't left with nothing. My husband and I put money into the caravan site - £14,000 of our own – and when my husband left we got the money back. And people who had homes that were used as Community houses got their houses back. So very few people were out of pocket."

Although, of necessity, the budget was limited, the ethos of the Community was far from austere. A lot of people have memories of parties and games and Viv says, "I had been brought up evangelical – no drink or dancing or make-up – and the first evening at Post Green, Tom Lees offered me a drink and I thought it would be a cup of coffee but he made me a cocktail, so I thought this was a bit different!

We left in the early 1980s. Things were a bit tense because the Community of Celebration and Post Green were going in different directions and also my daughters were 12 and 14 by then and I felt they needed a bit of normality. Some people had very deep problems and came specifically for healing, such as one girl with anorexia. Towards the end, my daughter said, 'Why does loving God cause so much pain?'

A Community member we were close to commuted from Bath and she suggested we went to live there. So we did, but stayed involved with the Community."

Households changed around, according to the needs of newcomers, with families and single people often sharing a home. Viv remembers one household as consisting of "my family and the mum and two small children from another family, and Christine and Marion, who were single."

So how did single people fare, living in this community of families and part-families, with people who were desperate for help and people who had committed their lives to helping?

STORY 9: SINGLE IN COMMUNITY

In his book, 'Another Man,' Tom Lees writes: "The spirit of the world is not a peaceable spirit. We are by nature self-indulgent, self-centred, greedy, insecure and fearful. These are the forces which control our lives and of which we are generally unconscious."

Being a single woman in our society is a status that is not always respected or considered desirable, so it might be thought that a measure of selfishness is one of the few perks of being single. But then, couples can also be selfish, and families may feel entitled to certain privileges 'for the sake of the children.'

So, given our natural human tendency to stake out our own territory in life and guard it for ourselves – whether for 'me' or for 'me and mine' – the challenge of community life is not easy for anyone.

How does it affect people coming into community as single individuals, alongside families who already form a little community in their own right?

Shirley, Marion and Christine recall their different experiences, but both Shirley and Christine mention that they didn't expect to be noticed or listened to, as single newcomers.

Shirley says, "I was quite an introvert before I joined the Community! You don't have to be extrovert to live in community. We had quite a strong leadership team and you had to embrace that, or it would be too difficult. They were people with more experience, deeper faith, and we had people from all over the world where things were done differently: the US, Australia, South Africa.

When I joined, there were 120 people in the Community and you couldn't have 120 people making decisions – and some people were only there for a short time - three months, six months or a year. I remember the time I found my voice, at some meeting, and I was quite surprised that people listened.

One of the things that drew me to the Community was how the children were treated, taken seriously. At mealtimes each person would say what they had been doing or what they were worried about, including the children. And there were lots of celebration days, fun days and parties with the children.

I was in the Community for six years, but have been a friend of the Community since 1975 when I came to my first youth camp at the age of 17, having become a Christian earlier that year.

Eventually I worked on the camp committee, running the young people's camps, and did the catering, in the old barn with two old cookers propped up on bricks – there was no Health and Safety then!

There were Breakaway camps for kids from urban areas like Deptford and Wolverhampton who had never seen a cow. They did problem-solving and team-building activities. One of the members in my household took the young people out making camps in the woods and Tom took them out on his boat. Viv was the camp nurse."

Career plans and work life had to be flexible in the Community, with members who were able to work and earn an income contributing to the living expenses of those who could not.

"The Community was involved in so much - publishing, a petrol station, fishing lakes, caravan park, shop, the Fisherfolk music business, evangelistic outreach, post office, camps – it kept growing. And some people were keeping the home, looking after children.

The Community was ahead of its time: no one had seen drama and music like that in worship before. After the split in 1986, we were all asked to choose which ministry we wanted to support – the music and outreach of the Community of Celebration or the pastoral ministry of Post Green. I stayed at Post Green and ran the Manpower Services *(temporary work agency)* unit in the village, and the people who were in counselling came and worked with me: we cut wood at Holton Lee for fires, made pottery and sold it at what is now the Courtyard Centre in Lytchett Minster, made candles, and also sold wholefoods with Faith."

There were times when Shirley struggled with decisions made by Community leaders, such as the time when a friend of hers who wanted to join was told she needed to go home for a while first and reconnect with her parents, against her own inclinations.

But overall, she says, "I wouldn't change it: I had my very best days and worst days in community. You have to work at your fellowship, if it's going to work, and with the children. I would probably do it all over again!"

Marion echoes Shirley's assessment of the challenges of living in community but she also loved the opportunity of being part of an extended 'family'.

"I loved the children; in each household I lived in, the parents were in charge of their own children but they would often invite someone to be someone special in the child's life, sit next to them at meals, and I was quite involved in the children's ministry at the camps.

It's not easy living with other people in a community but the good things were the worship and teaching and also that it felt like family – a home. We lived exactly as a normal family would.

We had prayers at 6.30am – which I didn't often attend! Breakfast was at 7.15, then about half an hour of chores: cleaning, laundry, preparing the evening meal.

Some people worked outside; I was asked to give up my job in a bank and take over the book-keeping for the Community and also for the Celebration Services publishing and Fisherfolk music. Some people were home-makers, and a couple ran our own crèche at one point, around 1976-7 when there were a lot of small children under four. Older children went off to local schools.

We went to St Dunstan's church at the end of each day, for a short chapel time, for sharing, dance and teaching. Children were involved and everyone came after work. Then we went back to the households for supper.

Most of us attended the parish church on a Sunday but there were some Catholics and other denominations who went to their own churches.

We had 50p pocket money a week, some of our food would be headed towards its sell-by date and when money was short we had to cut back on coffee and make our own marg, but we lived in quite lovely houses and had cars to use.

I've lived in probably most of the Community houses. We used to move fairly often; my longest stay in one place was probably two years and the shortest time four months. Single people had to do a lot of sharing of bedrooms.

The leadership group, which consisted of Tom, Faith, someone from the business side and people from the pastoral counselling side, made the decisions about where people lived. I was usually given a choice between two places when we moved."

New people coming into the Community for help with complex personal problems would be allocated a place in the household most suited to their needs. That meant that some of the people already living there had to move out - but in practice that meant that everybody moved!

Marion explains, "There would be a moving day, with vans going back and forth in the village. The only thing people would take with them was their own bed, if they wanted to! I might pack up all my belongings, go to work in the office all day, then come home to a different place."

Perhaps because of this practice, Shirley comments that she became very minimalist and in later life in her own home still has few possessions!

These comings and goings aroused some negative reactions from local villagers (we will hear from one long-standing resident, Thelma, shortly). Many viewed the Community with suspicion from the beginning, though Marion makes the point that a lot of Community members had individual friends in the village and wider locality, or were part of the parish church and the choir.

If shifting households caused disruption to neighbours and villagers, the frequent moves required even more adjustment from Community members.

"It was a sacrificial way of life," Marion admits. "Because we were a caring community, a lot of people came who had personal problems that made things very hard. There were difficulties as well in living with people from different backgrounds, countries, histories and cultures. There were silly arguments like whether to have roast potatoes or mashed on Christmas Day!"

Marion had first become introduced to the Post Green Community when she was 18. "Someone gave me a leaflet about the evening Bible College course and I decided to come. I was working in a bank and got a transfer to the area. I immediately loved the place.

I was at the Bible College for two years and got involved with the camps and conferences, and helped out a little bit with the rebuilding of East Holton farmhouse, which was a wreck.

In 1974, at the end of Bible College, I was invited to join the Community and I was in it for ten years. The first households were set up in 1974-5, then the Community of Celebration came to join us. By 1976-7, there were about 120 people living in the Community.

I am an easy-going, fun-loving person so my memories are a lot of the good times and the wonderful family. Other people may have some negative feelings. But one of the important things for me is what an impact the Community had on our lives."

Like Viv, Marion found that the decision for Post Green and the Community of Celebration to part, which was painful for many members, was also a positive opportunity to rethink her own future.

"I'd been part of it for 13 years in all and it was a time when I was thinking about my own life, so I decided to leave. But I've always kept in very close contact with both Communities. I look back on my time here with absolute fondness.

I went to work for a publishing company but the role was not really me, and I was looking to buy my own property so I needed a decent salary. I went back into banking, and I got married.

But it still feels like coming home when I come to Holton Lee. I can see from Livability newsletters that it's a continuation in some ways and I am proud of that. I do feel it's a lot of what Tom and Faith's vision was about."

Christine's perspective is different from both Shirley's and Marion's, in that she came to the Community later in life – at 29 rather than 17 or 18 as they did – and as a visitor from another country. She tells of her first impressions of Post Green.

"I was 29 when I came here from New Zealand in 1973. There was a group of people who prayed for me before I left, for God to send me to a group of Christians, and I thought that was strange as I didn't know any Christians in England! I was just coming for a working holiday.

After about a year in this country I came down to Post Green with a couple and their baby. They were coming for a ten-day New Year conference and I was the babysitter, looking after their baby, so not involved in the conference, which was not at Post Green House itself but over at South Lytchett Manor – the original manor house owned by the family, which is a school now.

I remember there was a list by the dining room door of all the attendees and I was just down as No. 18 – Babysitter. They didn't know my name, as I wasn't attending the conference. So I thought I would be on the edge. But I was hit by the love. I was treated as an equal, not as the babysitter at the bottom of the list.

I went back to Surrey where I was supply teaching, finished out the term then joined the Community in April, 1974.

My main work was for the Fisherfolk music business, in a house in Lytchett Minster village, in the sales department, packing. I had no office skills at that point.

In some ways, I had it easy. The people involved in the pastoral side had to deal with people slashing their wrists and jumping out of windows. The 'city of refuge' wasn't ordered: Tom and Faith had always had open house. It was Community members Carolyn and Gerry who really brought order and structured the Pastoral Centre."

Eventually the Pastoral Centre became based in Ash Tree Cottage on the Holton Lee site, though the farmhouse too was often a forum for counselling in a reassuringly normal environment.

Even without the immediate responsibility for dealing with personal crises among the people who came to Post Green for help, there were challenges in just living alongside people in everyday life.

"Lots of times in the Community it was difficult because you couldn't choose who you lived with. We lived in different households to support needy people, and we moved around quite a bit to meet those needs. There were conflicts, of course, and in that situation you couldn't just ignore it: whatever was blocking you in your relating to other people would be challenged. The rule was that if we couldn't work it out between ourselves, we would get a third person in to help.

People who came for healing or help tended to leave once they had that help, so there was always a fair amount of coming and going in the households.

As a single person in the Community, life was easier because we had no dependents. We were all in different circumstances and some of us didn't pay National Insurance, but Faith paid our pension contributions for us, for when we decided to leave.

There was a sacrificial side to community living. I gave the best years of my life to the Community, gave up sport and music, things I'd enjoyed before, because there was no money for sports kit or for going to concerts.

In 1990 I did a weekend course in therapeutic massage then trained in it for a year. The reason was because in Post Green Community there were plenty of warm, affirming hugs and I knew the healing power of touch and could see that offering massage would be a powerful, non-threatening, non-verbal way of bringing healing to people.

I also trained in horticulture and in 1995 I was involved in the transition from Post Green to Holton Lee, landscaping from the farmhouse to the other side of the Barn. It was a wasteland! The land wasn't farmed in the way it is now. The soil is very poor. It used to be much wilder here, with fewer footpaths – harder to get around.

I had moved out of Post Green by then. In 1994 I was about 50 and felt I needed to look at my long-term future, not dependent on the goodwill of Tom and Faith. At that time the government had a 50% ownership scheme so I was able to buy a place to live.

Things changed when Faith died in 1996. But the spirit of the place is on-going, with the people in the spinal unit and in Flourish and the main groups that use the place, like Dorset Forest Schools for children.

I don't feel I've ever really left the Community. Although I moved from Post Green House to Upton, one of the Community members lived in the same close as me. I was very busy as a self-employed gardener.

Then after four years I married Tom, in 1998. I wanted to come back and volunteer at Holton Lee, but Post Green was full-time. I continued to do the massage for six years, then stopped, because there was so much to do at Post Green. Tom and I eventually moved to a little cottage from Post Green House, which was too big for the two of us."

After Tom's death, Christine stayed living in the village. After a couple of years she became a contributor to recording the oral history of Holton Lee and began attending a weekly prayer meeting set up to support the work there; she remains a valuable link between the past and the future of the place.

STORY 10: COMMUNITY WITHIN COMMUNITY

Thelma is a long-term resident of Lytchett Minster, the village of which Post Green is a part, and is the owner of the beautiful little thatched shop selling antiques and the traditional stitched Dorset buttons. With connections in the village as well as friends in the Post Green Community, she is well placed to comment on local people's reactions to the presence of a therapeutic Christian Community in their midst.

"My family moved down from Yorkshire to Dorset in 1947, in a car with a trailer – with a chicken in the back, sitting on some eggs! We had a caravan on Lady Lees' site in Lytchett Minster and used to let it out and go and clean it, and I had seen a little shop there that was all derelict and I went to see Sir Tom and asked if we could rent it. Tom said they would do the floor if we did the rest. It was damp, with ivy growing under the tiles, but we thought it would make a splendid antique shop. My mum used to go to house auctions and buy all the leftover junk at the end and I had learned about antiques without realising. I got the feel for it.

It was Tom's idea to give us the buttons to sell. In 1900 Florence, Lady Lees, his grandmother, collected them. Dorset button-making started in 1650 and went on till 1851 when the Crystal Palace Exhibition showed a button-making machine, which killed the industry. Lady Florence tried to restart it, in this little shop and a thatched shed across the road.

I've been in Lytchett now for 48 years. The shop has never been terribly busy; there wasn't much money in it and we didn't sell many of the old buttons, but I took them and went around and gave talks about them and I've been able to enthuse people about the craft. I've produced kits and written a book.

At 84, I'm still doing talks to WI and school groups and I open the shop in the afternoons from Tuesday to Friday and on Saturday mornings. It has always been a hobby but a delightful one: it has made my life.

I became aware of the Post Green Community shortly after I started the shop in 1970 and I watched it grow. The Community members started to come to the church and they were considered very avant-garde: at the Sign of Peace they would all get up and kiss one another. Everybody does it now and thinks nothing of it but the church then was very traditional.

Sometimes the Community people used to wander round the church and play guitar in the corner. In the beginning, a lot of people came into the Community because they were troubled, and their behaviour could be strange. I was walking to the shop from Sandy Lane one misty morning and suddenly this vision appeared of a man who looked just like Christ, in a gown, with long hair and a beard, and he walked past and didn't see me. It gave me such a shock!

The reaction of local people was to stop going to church. No one had travelled anywhere at that time and a lot of people were in their 80s so the Community was quite a shock to the village, with people from all different nationalities and with different ways coming into it.

Even when I first started the shop, village people were reticent: they would walk past and look in the window but it was three or four years before they started coming in.

I got to know Faith and I understood her idea but to the village the Community was like another culture.

I was glad about the Post Green Community; I could see what they were doing and I used to chat to Faith about it. I was never overawed by people and I used to go up to Post Green House sometimes and sit in the kitchen, and I would take them lemon curd at Easter. Faith had had cancer on her ears and had to have part removed. When she died, I did the flowers for her funeral. Tom was always involved in village life so he was aware of the effect of the Community on the village. I had a young man working for me who had been in the Post Green Community and when the Community ended he was at a loss. He couldn't read or write and I needed help in the shop so I gave him a job.

There were good things that came out of the Post Green Community for the village. People gradually came back to church and they got used to the changes. When they came back, it was a different place, much warmer and friendlier. After Post Green, the pews went and the chairs came in instead and now we have a vicar who makes people feel at home, and I think that's a spin-off from Post Green."

It's clear that emotional health involves participation in community and that no one can become wholeheartedly well by receiving individual help while remaining isolated from society.

But the same is true of communities. As Thelma confirms, any community needs to work within the context of its neighbourhood and locality. Even communities that are strong in themselves need wider connections if they are to stay healthy and not become insular or detached from reality.

Shirley Walker, activities and events organiser at Holton Lee, gives her view of how this works - and why it needs to be worked at, even when an organisation's resources are limited and staff are already busy.

"Links with the local community are probably based first on mutual need: in our case, social agencies need to send people to us and we need referrals from them. But community is much more than that.

There's a need to foster connections with the neighbourhood, its schools, businesses, churches and other charities, and to be more reciprocal. For instance, we advertise other organisations' job vacancies on our social media and publicise their fundraising events or give them space at our own.

Holton Lee has the advantage of already having a diverse community working within the site, with all the day courses we provide and various projects run by other organisations, as well as facilities hired by different groups, and the grounds used by birdwatchers, walkers, people using the exercise trail and camping groups.

It does require effort to ensure that no single group assumes ownership or exclusive rights over communal facilities. But the benefits of sharing far outweigh the occasional tensions.

Then, of course, Livability is a community in itself, with schools, colleges, disability care units and community projects across the UK."

Neil Stevens, aft   ur years' management at Holton Lee and now
working on stra   and planning at Livability's national office,
finds that staff   ing at the charity's 35 various UK sites are
united by their   ion for empowering people but separated by
geography.

"It needs som   re thought still to find ways of connecting those
staff with one   ther, to recognise how much they have in
common. Ar   helpful to look at how the experience of people
at Holton L   ding something better out of life by being here,
could be re   d in other environments, for example, in an
urban setti

One of Li   y's community partners and link churches is a
church in   nham which, as well as providing worship space for
a number   urch congregations, also hosts a pre-school, sports
club and   on a site enclosed by four major roads, so that's
obvious   ry different environment but provides people with a
similar   of space in their lives."

It may   as though that's quite enough community to be going
on wit'   why go looking for more involvement in the local
area, r   ally and online; wouldn't busy staff tend to see that as
extra   on-essential work?

"Bei   wider community is always better," Shirley explains. "We
can   rt and learn from one another. I've seen how effective it
can   en organisations co-operate – and how wasteful it is
wh   e replicates what someone else is already doing in the
sar   d. Whether they're competing or are just unaware of the
wo   at others are doing, it causes bad feeling.

When I was involved in children's work, there were some very
good local projects but once, on two consecutive weekends,
different children's workers organised two very similar events
without either of them knowing what the other one was planning!
We try to have a presence in the local business network, at NHS
meetings, with county community action groups and at events for
local charities, as well as inviting the public to open days, spring
and Christmas markets and the annual Community Fair, where a
wide range of local craftspeople and organisations are represented.
Social media helps to keep us connected, as well as ordinary
publicity like signs on the roadside. But still, a lady who had lived
in the nearest village for 50 years told me recently she had no idea
this place existed or what went on here, so we still have some way
to go to make ourselves known!

The need to foster goodwill in the wider community is ongoing and the results are probably long-term, though sometimes there's an instant response, say to a Facebook request for donations of craft items or a bag of compost when supplies are low. And businesses sometimes send volunteer groups to carry out a particular project, like building a canopy for the outdoor oven. In our local area there are several other places doing similar projects but they're all slightly different or are for different age groups.

We've worked with groups of pupils with learning disabilities from schools and local colleges, and people from care homes, who come to try out new skills and experiences and interact with other people. But because the organisations have to provide their own transport and send staff to accompany the groups, recent funding cuts mean that some can't come any more.

Bournemouth Football Club ran PE classes for a local Livability education centre, and Bournemouth Symphony Orchestra did some music workshops with them. It's a good example of different local communities coming together. It's healthy; it benefits everyone.

Like the tide coming in on the harbour shore, all communities benefit from a flow of fresh people as well as the familiar faces of those who stay."

STORY 11: TIMES OF CHANGE

It's only fair to say that not everyone who was part of Holton Lee in its Post Green Community days feels that it has fulfilled Tom and Faith Lees' original vision as a centre of education and healing and refuge. A few feel that the element of Christian faith has been sidelined, despite being part of a Christian charity now. So we'll listen to Rob, who voices that view:

"I went to Post Green years ago as a young Christian, then my job took me elsewhere. When I came back from retirement, Tom Lees was quite an old man; it was others who picked up the process of change.

My role was as an event organiser for the Connect conferences in 2010, 2011 and 2013. I got excited about Connect, with the Christian programme, the involvement of local churches, and also with the sense of the history of the place: God's Spirit in a place where the Kingdom can come. Connect was the second phase.

I was chaplain at Lee Abbey for a time and when I came up the drive at Holton Lee there was the same feel about the place. Some people call it a 'thin place.' I describe it as 'deposits of glory,' the legacy passed on in the DNA of the place – in this case, the care, love, openness and acceptance of people – that remains for those who come afterwards to pick up the strands.

That legacy went into the doldrums. The need for secular funding brings with it health and safety issues, the need for people to be qualified and to have special equipment. There's less of the presence of hands-on healing ministry; it becomes a business."

Others would agree that the proliferation of health and safety requirements and the demand for professional qualifications in every field may have put restraints on the freedom of past practices – but would not agree that this turns divine healing into a purely secular, human concern, let alone a business venture.

Neil Stevens says that for him, as former site manager at Holton Lee, it was a relief to find that becoming part of Livability was not, as some had feared, an experience of a larger organisation imposing its own ethos or methods but a realisation that the organisations already shared the same heart.

"The passion for people is evident, from Post Green days until now as part of Livability, and so is the grassroots ethos that everyone is an inherently valuable human being because we are all created by the same God. That's still what drives everyone to want to bring people together. It's not to get something from them or do something to them but to equip them to live in the best way possible, helping each other to thrive through good relationships and to connect back into their communities, families, workplaces, wherever.

"It can't be the same formula for everybody, because we are all different. It depends what the individual wants out of life. To gain confidence to get back to work or to learn skills to help with daily life are very different goals. For some, that enhanced life may mean being helped to get out more into the world while for others it may be to have solitude, but not isolation, to develop their interest in art. Community means something different for everyone."

Increasing legislation and financial restraints may have played a part in the change of plans at Holton Lee but the requirements of service users themselves may also be a motivation for change in the way that services are provided.

Neil explains, "The Barn was set up as a respite centre for people with disabilities and their carers but with shared rooms, which is not acceptable now. And in the past, people recovering from spinal injuries would spend a very long time in hospital, which gave them time to learn wheelchair skills and for provision to be made for going home. Now they may spend as little as three months in hospital after a major injury, after which they are medically fit to go home but face all kinds of practical and social challenges – mobility, work, accessible facilities at home.

So with Livability the decision was taken to develop the Barn as a recovery unit for people with spinal injuries. And the two cottages at Holton Lee, originally accommodation for Post Green Community members and later holiday cottages for people with disabilities and their families, have now been upgraded with good wet-rooms and hoists and other equipment for people in wheelchairs. So they are now used as accessible holiday accommodation but could also be used for someone ready to leave the spinal injury unit to try out living on their own, or having family to stay, before they go home.

It's a question of listening to changing needs and trying to provide what people want now."

Two of Faith and Tom's children, Sarah and Bridget, are in a unique position to assess the vision of their parents, the changes and challenges that occurred along the way, and the working out of that vision in the present conditions of the 21st century. Sarah recalls her own impressions of Holton Lee and the Community, past and present:

"My earliest recollections of Holton Lee are of camping there as a child. We'd camp by the railway, watching the trains go past and having so much fun. It was a break from our parents and we'd go on walks and cook over camp fires.

Much later, after the Community was established, my husband and I would send our children to the annual camps here. So the children came camping too – but a different sort of camping with lots of activities for various age groups. They enjoyed the freedom of not having us around.

Long before the days of theCommunity, living at Post Green, we were used to being surrounded by other people. As a child I recall going to Scotland every year for our holidays and there would always be cousins or children of friends. My parents were extremely hospitable and were always bringing in people; cooking for huge numbers never fazed my mother - she had trained as a Cordon Bleu chef and was an excellent cook.

We were also used to being in the midst of crowds and groups of people through the films my grandmother made in the village. As little children all of us got involved in these films ('A Voice Crying in the Wilderness' and 'Messiah'), playing characters such as shepherds, and my mother was assistant director and would also take part. It was hard work. My grandmother even brought in camels from the local circus!

My parents always wanted to share what they had. They brought us all up to realise just how very privileged we all were and how important it was to share what we had been given with others. If any of us ever got bossy or thought we were superior to other people we were quickly and thoroughly told off!

I was at university when Jean Darnall, an American evangelist, arrived, and her arrival formalised things. I came back in 1977, got a job in Dorset and lived for six months at our family home, Post Green House.

I remember my parents and others continually supporting and helping people who were suicidal, bulimic, anorexic or hurting in some way. They were so far ahead of common practice and beliefs at the time.

The concept of Holton Lee was born at one of the camps. Howard and Jodi were living in the farmhouse and my mother was looking for ways to utilise the site to help people living with disabilities. I was working at SHAPE (an arts and disability organisation) at the time and my mother thought I should be involved, long before I was a trustee.

Post Green had been based on the concept of a city of refuge; she had the idea that they could create such a 'city' here at Holton Lee. Her idea was that it would outlive Post Green, providing a means of employment for the Community by creating jobs for people, rather than them being dependent on the Lees.

When my father who was in his late 70s said he wanted to slow down a little and withdraw from being actively involved at Holton Lee, I became Chair of Trustees. Learning on the job, I realised the importance of good, supportive trustees. There were good times and challenging moments too, with some different visions among different directors, managers and trustees.

However, Holton Lee is something very special; one member called it a 'sacred space.' There has always been a focus on nurturing, healing and loving people, expressed through creativity, the arts, the environment, personal growth and spirituality.

The Flourish project is wonderful! It's very exciting and I'd like to see more. People were blessed and continue to be blessed by Holton Lee."

Sarah's younger sister, Bridget, also gives her personal perspective of the sometimes rocky journey from the original vision to present day practice:

"We're a big family – I'm one of four and Dad was one of eight children. In our family, the elder son inherits and the girls are supposed to marry well – or not! Dad's elder brother, my Uncle James, was meant to inherit but he died so it passed to Dad - Tom. As a teenager, Tom asked the gamekeeper to tell him about the wildlife at Holton. The gamekeeper told him to sit on a log and listen, and he became aware of all the life going on around him.

I remember, before the Post Green community existed, there were always people staying with us at Post Green House, people in need. My mother was really into rebuilding people, including people who had been abused, helping them find their confidence again.

In 1967 I was 13 and my mother had a breakdown and spent time at the home of a clergyman and his wife. It wasn't a community but it was a time of renewal in the Church and they were involved in it.

My father had always been a deep-rooted Christian and an altruistic man whereas Mum was on the practical side of life, looking after the family. But once they were both committed as Christians – 'born again' – they wondered what to do about it.

Jean Darnall and her daughter moved into the house with us – she had a charismatic character. Her daughter, LaDonna, was about a year older than me and we became friends. Jean was a godsend to us, and we were to her because she was frazzled. Elmer, her husband, came later and he started up the Bible college with Dad and Mum and others, which ran from about 1969 to 1974.

Other people who became involved were the leaders of the Church of the Redeemer in Houston, Texas, out of which grew the Fisherfolk music ministry, and they started the Community of Celebration in the UK. Jodi was a member of the Fisherfolk. My parents got to be very good friends with them and wanted to support their ministry.

In 1972 I moved in with the Community of Celebration, when I came out of hospital after a long stay: I had a serious motorbike accident and was nearly killed. My left arm was crushed and needed a lot of time to mend; it still doesn't work very well. I thought I ought to move out of home but, in time, the Community of Celebration moved closer to Post Green.

I left when I got married in 1975 but the Community continued. That was the same year Mum got kidney cancer and nearly died.

I liked the fact that Post Green bridged denominations: members were Elim Pentecostal, Catholic, there was a Baptist minister, and my dad was on the General Synod of the Anglican Church.

At first, I think my father had financed everything. Then, there was a common purse – I think until the late 1980s - and some people had jobs. The fundraising towards building Holton Lee started around the time of the 25th anniversary of Post Green.

We didn't know what to call the place at first. People think the 'Lee' in Holton Lee is because of the name of the family but it was chosen because it's a sailing term. Lee means protection, a place of shelter. A ship in a storm pulls into the lee of an island.

My mother died just after Holton Lee was opened, in 1996. Faith House was built a long time later, so it wasn't named as a memorial to her name, 'Faith'; it just described what it was.

My sister Sarah was Chairperson. When we applied for planning permission for Faith House, one of the plans we liked best was for a series of little pods – where the Flourish centre is now – which included a chapel. In the event, we thought Faith House, with its attached Quiet Room with the silver birch trunks inside, was like a chapel itself.

Most of the Americans from the Community of Celebration went back to the States and some of the English went with them. But members of the Post Green Community still get together and there's a Facebook page. My father's sister, Jane, still runs a Bible study – at 91!

We couldn't afford the constraints of keeping Holton Lee going any more and that's when Livability came in. My sister Sarah was very much involved in the changeover.

I sold my little house in Lytchett Minster village nine years ago and my husband and I went travelling; now we're back in Dorset.

I feel peaceful about Holton Lee being Livability now. It's still being used by people with disabilities, and we are all disabled in some ways – and all perfect!"

Another family member who feels that Holton Lee today expresses Tom and Faith's vision for the future is their grandson, John, who has encountered disability issues with perseverance and faith and is now an enthusiastic Flourish participant. Here is his experience: "I've been coming here for nine years, and before that I had heard people talk about Flourish; I knew it was here. I was doing gardening at home and liked it, and at college I did horticulture and I came here straight after college. I'm 26 now.

I see Flourish as a nice working area. The purpose of the project is to help people with disabilities. Coming here has helped me to be more outside, in the garden environment. I like being outside but left to myself I would probably be indoors more.

I usually do watering or weeding – because it needs doing and because it's what I like – and I like planting. In fact, I like everything!

At school I was always very bad at Maths but good at the spelling and languages side – French and German. I was at school in France. We lived there from when I was nine to when I was 16, coming and going - there for the semesters and back here for the holidays.

I learned to ski from a young age, because we were in the Alps, near Chamonix. I like ski-ing, mainly cross-country because you don't get the same amount of people as with downhill ski-ing so you don't get squished!

I have an elder sister, two younger sisters and a younger brother. We get on well: when there's five of you, there's not much choice! I liked growing up in a big family. It enhances your character, makes you more cheerful and happy.

I had dyspraxia and it affected my co-ordination and made me impractical. My hands weren't responsive and it made it difficult to do practical things. When I tried to carry things I used to drop them.

I have faith in God, mainly through my grandfather. I was close to him and I saw a lot of him. He didn't really talk about his faith but he was a kind person and I think I got my faith from him. I am a kind person as well.

When I came here I found being with people very easy and I've made friends. I've seen other people come through Flourish and come out a different person. One girl has got more used to noise: it used to upset her a lot and it doesn't now.

I have changed by coming here. I'm more responsible than I was before. I can see what needs doing and get on with it, on my own – though you are never on your own here; there's always someone there.

If somebody asked me, I could describe where everything is in the garden; it's like a map inside my head. There's a family connection to the place but I would be drawn to it anyway. I feel happy when I come up the drive.

The spirit of the place is what you could call mindful. Mindfulness is using your senses and it's very sensory here, with all the plants and the garden.

I would say to other people that they could definitely make their life better and less difficult by coming into the garden.

My confidence was down there – low – when I first came here but now I know where I am and I know who I am.

I think the low confidence came from other people. I had a low opinion of myself, probably because I didn't have many friends. There was a bit of bullying at school – not really bad but it made me unconfident about seeing people and speaking out.

Here, from the first day, people were very nice. They showed interest in me and encouraged me to be myself. That's the way the staff are with other people, and the way people are with each other. People with severe disabilities are treated the same as everyone else. That fits in with the way I am, and with the way I like to treat people.

My confidence and self-esteem gradually came up. I come to Flourish three days a week now. It went from one day a week to two days, then three, because I was enjoying it. And on other days I do gardening at home.

I've learned a lot, things you couldn't learn on a course at college, like building a Hugel bed. Katrina (a staff member) and I had the idea and Katrina researched it and then we built it up from the research. A Hugel bed is built on top of wood and compost and manure and it's quite good for growing squashes and courgettes. I've helped out at open days and fairs and that's something I would have found difficult before but now I don't.

From the first of August, on Tuesdays, I will come here to do land maintenance, as a paid job. I'm looking forward to it."

STORY 12: GAME-CHANGERS

Personal experience of Holton Lee has led some people to change their priorities and even their career or retirement plans.

Les and his wife Pam moved from another area of the country to be part of the Post Green Community's planned expansion to Holton Lee in the 1990s, and Les took up a new post-retirement career as a carer.

Alan, having attended Flourish to help him recover from a second stroke, became well enough to return to work as a builder, but found himself reviewing the person he was before and deciding on a new path.

Ron, from being a teacher, was forced by his stroke into dependency and having to relearn the most basic skills, but at Holton Lee he not only recovered a sense of peace but discovered a new usefulness for his connection with wildlife and nature.

And Mike, told he had no time at all left to live, discovered new depths of talent and compassion in volunteering.

Here are the stories of people who jumped out of the categories of career and social roles, as a result of getting to know some of the extraordinary people whom society overlooks. And in doing so, they became extraordinary themselves.

Here's Les, first of all:

"In 1981 I was married to Pam, with three daughters aged teenage, six and four, living in Epsom, attending a church that emphasised church as community: the vicar familiarised the congregation with active Christian communities – L'Arche, L'Abri and Post Green. I remember a sermon one time, in another church, being told that Jesus was 33 – and I was 33 at the time – and that he died for you … and you, and *you*. It was personal.

The parish holiday was camping at Post Green and our family was impressed by the great welcome. Despite some initial reservations about camping, we kept coming every year.

In the early 1990s, Faith Lees' vision was to build the charity by creating a small village of cabins at Holton Lee for people to stay for a short or longer time, but by 1992-3 funding had dried up so the decision was made to build the new Barn to accommodate nine people with disabilities. This opened in 1996.

We were still living in Epsom at that time, where I had been working for the Royal Mail for 30 years as a manager, but I was coming and going to Holton Lee and helping with fundraising.

In 1997, Holton Lee had a stand at an exhibition in Bournemouth and I got talking to someone from Cheshire Homes, who told me I would make a good carer. I wanted to do something different in retirement.

In 2006 I went to work for the Shaftesbury Society (which later merged with John Grooms Association for the Disabled to become Livability) for 18 months. I was doing residential work with young people from their late teens to early 30s.

I loved care work but it was tough at times. I was a key-worker for a young woman with multiple sclerosis and breathing difficulties. She had a Do Not Resuscitate notice, which I found really hard to handle, in such a young person, so I left, six weeks before she died. I worked for six months at Bournemouth Churches Housing Association with homeless youngsters, then for Dorset County Council doing home care for the elderly, till the council handed over to an outside company.

I was still volunteering in the garden and on site at Holton Lee, and Pam had been working in the garden there right from the beginning and then helped with catering, on a small scale.

What has lasted of the original vision? Faith said, 'If we don't act out what we say, we are not achieving anything.' My feeling is that it has developed for the better, because it's a recognised Christian charity. I think that Livability taking over is the best thing that could have happened to the Community vision. Originally, the Community was fundraising to build a chapel at Holton Lee but instead we have Faith House, which is open for use by groups in the local community. And a few Christians in this area, including me, are trying to introduce the idea of eco-Church – a Church that's more environmentally aware and eco-friendly, the way things are at Holton Lee.

Some outsiders don't understand what the Community was all about and what it was trying to do, and thought it was some sort of weird sect. But the Community didn't want to just go and be spiritual; they wanted to be community *with* people.

That's what drew us to it, and it's what's still happening here. More recently, I've been asked to help in the office, so that's another change for me. And it's fine."

Les made changes to his lifestyle and work voluntarily, as he felt prompted by God and encouraged or invited by other people. By contrast, Alan had life-changes forced on him by circumstances. He, and the others, are proof that you don't have to be damaged to be a volunteer – but sometimes it helps!

"I've met a lot of people in the same boat as me. I've had two major brain haemorrhages, one eight years ago and one just over three years ago.

I was really depressed after the second stroke; I was that much older – 62 - and having to learn to walk again. I felt like I didn't want to live. I had been so active: I ran a boxing gym for a long time, and as a self-employed house builder I was a workaholic, obsessed with getting money. The building trade is cut-throat.

I was going to physio after the second stroke and someone came around the house and asked if I wanted to go to Holton Lee. I didn't really have much feeling about anything and to start with it took a lot of effort to come here – but within two weeks I loved it. Everyone was so friendly. And I thought, 'What have I got to be depressed about?' It woke me up.

I've known people who have had strokes who sit at home and vegetate but you can retrain the brain. You've got to keep as active as you can. The brain is never going to heal up but you can train it like a little kid: you can learn to do things again but you have got to keep working at it.

I was a little bit nervous when I first came to Flourish but after having a cup of tea with everybody, I thought, 'What am I here for?' Some people were ten times worse off than me. There were people with learning disabilities, people in wheelchairs.

It was good for me to work with them. It got me out of that greedy, money-money frame of mind. As time went by and I was getting better, I started doing work around the place.

I left Flourish to go back to work but after a while I started getting back into my old ways and I started getting anxiety again. So I've come back to Holton Lee and the anxiety has all drifted away because I enjoy it so much.

Working with the young guys, we've made garden furniture and I've made bird-boxes so the guys can just screw them together and there's something they've made.

I appreciate seeing the boys learning things. It helps them and it helps me, and that's worth more than money."

Ron also had to face the humiliation of losing his independence and many of the abilities we take for granted, and to change his perception of life and of himself.

A retired biology teacher who had a stroke in 2001, Ron has been coming to Holton Lee since the earliest days of the gardening project and has deep roots in the Flourish programme!

"I needed to come here. I've always been interested in nature and wildlife and growing things but after my stroke I didn't feel like myself any more: I had lost my speech and my ability to write, which was a part of my identity as a teacher. I had also lost confidence, especially socially, and even now I find it difficult if I'm at the rugby club or somewhere and a group of four or five people are all talking at once.

After the stroke I had physio and occupational therapy. My mobility was good enough to do weeding and potting on, and I had kept my memory of plants, especially vegetable growing, so a social worker suggested I came to Holton Lee. It was just a small garden then, about half an acre, with two polytunnels and a greenhouse that kept being blown away in storms and eventually wasn't replaced.

There were just two or three of us to start with. I was coming once a week, funded by Dorset County Council, and also started doing a computer course in Wareham to get back my skills, as well as having physio and speech therapy. Recovering from a stroke is hard work, tiring and humiliating – learning to speak and write again and just to be with people.

But Holton Lee is a nice place, surrounded by nature and wildlife and so many birds – I've recorded 156 species since I've been here – and gradually my confidence came back. I've got back my speech and my writing has reverted to the way it was – my signature is still the same, which for me is a sign that I'm still the same person.

My funding ended in 2005 but I became a volunteer and I've been here 17 years now. I mainly work in the greenhouse, and I still use my old dissecting kit from the biology labs, which is great for sowing seeds!"

The turnaround in Mike's life was something that nobody expected, least of all himself, when he was told he was going to die or else be left in a vegetative state.

"I was a self-employed builder but when I was 54 I had an inoperable brain tumour that burst and I couldn't work or drive any more. I lost the pension I was building up and nearly lost my house as well.

It knocks you for six because you feel useless. After I came out of hospital I was just stuck at home.

My wife and a lady from Social Services were looking for places I could go and I said I wasn't going to do painting or pottery! But they came and had a look around Holton Lee and I thought it sounded OK.

I started in 2016 and at first I came once a week. My first impression was that it was nice, good to get out of the house, and the people were friendly, though it took me a long time to connect with people and not to switch off when they were talking.

When a scan showed my brain had got worse, I said I wasn't coming in any more. But some of those boys here are worse off than me – even though they can use a mobile phone and I can't! I can't feel sorry for myself.

Being around people with different disabilities has shown me that there are people out there – thousands – getting on with life when it's difficult. I look at people in a different way now; I see people as people, not as a disability.

I wasn't particularly keen on the gardening side: I've got plenty of gardening at home. But then I started making things out of wood. I had a lot of experience of working with wood, as a builder, and that skill side of my brain wasn't affected, though my memory was. Here, at Flourish, there's no pressure to do anything; you can try things and see what you like. But I don't really mind what I do here. It's a lovely place: the people are nice and the place itself is beautiful. For the past eight months, I've been coming here three days a week as a trained volunteer.

In November I went for a hospital appointment and the doctor said my brain had got worse, but he couldn't understand how I was doing the things I am doing. He said the work I'm doing here at Flourish is better than any medication and told me to keep going! I like teaching the young lads and helping them get a sense that they can do things, so they'll be able to move on. If they can take a wheel off and put it back on, they may start thinking they could make a good mechanic; you don't need to be good at reading and writing.

We could do more here but it all costs money. They're fundraising to build a big barn, with one area as a mechanical workshop. We could teach the young people skills by doing up an old car. Then they could see they'd achieved something. I'd like to be part of that."

Mike and Alan are now an essential part of Flourish, always on hand to fix fences or gates or build vegetable cages in the garden, making wooden items for sale and teaching group members to use tools and develop woodworking and mechanical skills.

It takes courage to embrace change in your own life. It's a risk to leave the comfort zone – even when every comfort zone has become uncomfortable. But the sacrifice pays off.

STORY 13: GOING THE EXTRA MILE

Christine Lees mentioned the sacrificial side to living in a community that exists to benefit outsiders, and an element of sacrifice accompanies any effort to stand against the tide of culture, which rejects all categories of people it considers unproductive. It's this effort to challenge perceptions, as well as the everyday demands of practical care, that requires parents, carers, teachers, social workers, health professionals and project leaders, to go the extra mile for the sake of people with disabilities and unrecognised abilities.

Funding and the lack of it continues to block the way forward for many vital projects but individuals can make a remarkable difference. For athlete Pete Thompson it was a growing awareness of mental health issues and his work with elderly people living with dementia, as well as his questioning of his own priorities, that led him to a unique way of 'going the extra mile.'

In 2017, at the age of 32, he ran the equivalent distance of 44 marathons – 1,153 miles - in 44 European countries in 44 consecutive days.

Then in 2018, seven weeks ahead of the Tour de France cyclists, he ran the entire Tour de France route – 2,069 miles - finishing ahead of the riders. From both challenges, hoping to raise £10,000 for Flourish and for the mental health charity Mind, he raised £50,000.

Here Pete tells his story:

"I have family members who suffer from depression and anxiety. Then when I was 19 and at university studying education, I had a girlfriend who had body dysmorphic disorder. She was attractive and came across as confident but she couldn't see in the mirror what other people saw: she saw herself as hideously ugly.

People thought it was vanity; they didn't understand. She got different therapies, which sometimes helped and sometimes didn't.

It was really hard to see someone I cared about not want to leave the house, or have to put on so much make-up in order to do so. I wanted to help but I felt helpless and inevitably it affected our relationship.

I have also had other girlfriends with depression and bipolar, who would often battle with the decision on whether or not to take the medication they had been prescribed. The thought that it stopped them being themselves and took away a piece of them was something I could completely understand. I would try and do what I thought best but it was incredibly difficult and frustrating to not know what to advise or suggest for the best and I don't know if I always got that right.

I've seen the real impact of serious mental illness on someone's life. There is definitely still a stigma about mental health. It's great that people are now talking about it but there's a danger of mental illness being normalised, casually using terms like 'depression' for periods of frustration or sadness. Or phrases like 'I'm a little OCD' when for example talking about the need to place their mugs in the cupboard in a certain order. It is something I hear all the time and it really annoys me.

For me, my worst experience was probably a six-month period after a relationship break-up. I was unhappy and really struggled to deal with things but I wouldn't equate that with the suffering that people with mental illness go through on a daily basis, some every day of their lives.

 The numbers of people who die by suicide, however, are not just due to mental illness; a person can have a mental illness and good mental health and vice versa, so those feelings definitely need to be heard and for people to be encouraged and supported to share them.

I'm not 100 percent sure where the conversation about mental health is going at the moment. By getting people to be more open about it, more can be done to help and that is of course a really positive thing, but if everybody feels they suffer from depression, that doesn't help with understanding the difference between normal stress and serious illness.

There needs to be a better understanding of the more extreme end of the scale, which may make people feel uncomfortable to see or read about, but education on the issue is incredibly important.

When my relationship broke down a few years ago, I found it very hard to accept and had a lot of unanswered questions. I wanted and needed something to blame, and I blamed the focus I had placed on my running for ruining the relationship, so I decided to give it up. Long distance running is very absorbing and when I was building up to a big race – about every six months - I was incredibly focused on it. It had become an identity: people knew me as a runner and I enjoyed being congratulated on winning.

I started running at the age of 23. Before that I played football and county level short tennis and had always been competitive about sport but I never had any interest in running. But my brother, who's a couple of years older than me, got interested and then a friend and I started, and signed up for a local race. I wasn't that good at running – just never gave up! I came from being placed number 50 in cross-country to winning it. I liked the idea of a challenge and I applied for the ballot for the London Marathon a few times.

During that difficult six months when I blamed myself for the relationship break-up and turned away from running, I realised that for my own mental health I needed the clear focus that running gave me, as well as the enjoyment of seeing friends and getting to travel, through races. I've always enjoyed work but liked to have something outside work as well.

So I decided I needed to get back into running, but to get it back the right way. I came up with the idea of doing it to raise awareness and funds for charity to give me a new motivation, not just running for personal goals or fitness. I ran the London Marathon in 2010 for Mind, because it is a leading mental health charity, though I didn't have a personal involvement with it as I now have with Flourish.

For the 44 marathons in 44 countries in 44 days challenge, I sometimes had someone join me for part of the run but I was on my own for most of the time, including all the travelling. I was running to raise funds for a community, Flourish, but the process was solitary.

The trip took about six months of meticulous planning; without that, it couldn't have worked. For example, I knew that, six days in, very tired, I would need that crib sheet that I had meticulously planned, so that I would know the route to walk from the train station to the next hotel and where I was going to run the following day. If I'd just bodged it as I went along I would have fallen apart.

I had a Plan B for every stage of the journey, which was all by public transport. There were some things I couldn't control, like a night bus from Bosnia to Croatia that just didn't run, and islands like Malta and Iceland that had one plane out and that was it, so I had to get there on time!

People assumed that travelling between the marathons would be rest time but planes and coaches are a confined space and you can't stretch your muscles or elevate your feet when they swell. My feet were disgusting: I couldn't wave them in the air, with other passengers around!

Because I was doing the challenge to raise awareness and funds for the charities, I was keeping people updated on social media and doing a video diary. To really hit high levels of fundraising depends on how much media coverage you get so this was my way of trying to spread the word.

I didn't have a PR team or time to send emails to TV stations; the video diary was all I did. But at times when I didn't talk to anyone for three or four days it was also therapeutic to know I was talking to people in some way, and the messages I was getting back from people were a huge motivation to keep going.

People from Flourish sent messages and made a video of service-users 'running a mile with Pete' and it was a really encouraging reminder that I was part of a community, not doing this for myself or on my own.

The Tour de France challenge was easier in some ways because the route was set and also because my girlfriend, Sally, did the whole route with me, in a support car, which made an incredible difference.

After the two challenges, there was some press attention and TV appearances, which inspired people to donate and also to think about doing something themselves. I am naturally quite a shy person but I'm happy to be asked to share my story and to be part of the conversation about mental health.

As well as being aware of mental health issues through my experience of relationships and some of my friends – one of whom suffers from anorexia and another with personality disorder - my work has given me more awareness. I began as a careers advisor and then worked in support services at a college, and now work in social prescribing.

The idea of social prescribing is to support people to engage in community activities. So someone going to the doctor regularly, like an elderly person already receiving medical help but living quite an isolated life, can get a social prescription. We were set up to help elderly people but recently there have been more referrals for people of all ages with mental health problems.

That's how I first came across Flourish, in 2015 when I came to see if it might help some of the people I was working with. I would come here with them the first time or come back later to see how they were getting on.

It was a perfect place for some people. Going anywhere new for the first time is very difficult for anyone who is struggling with everyday life but there's a huge welcome here – and you certainly don't get that everywhere! It comes from the staff setting that example, then that feeds into everyone else.

The beauty of this place is something very hard to describe: it's not just the natural environment but a community who really care about each other and get on with each other. When you come here you are made to feel part of something, and the people I was working with didn't have that anywhere else.

Being an outsider is one of the worst feelings in the world. It's hard enough starting a new job – but if you feel like that all the time ….!

It's hard for many people to be open about their feelings. I find that since doing the challenges people have been more open with me about their sufferings. Everybody has times when they struggle and don't know how to deal with certain things.

Of my friends, initially only one asked why I was going to do the challenges for mental health charities, and I realised I had never spoken to them about that six months of feeling so unhappy. Even now, I have a tendency to want to try to deal with things by myself but I know that's not the best thing to do.

Places like Flourish clearly work because they help so many people and you can see the change in them. It's quite a simple idea, having a garden where people come and work. You could do something similar with sporting or art-based activities. But it's not easy.

To get people to be open, there has to be the support available when they do open up and talk. They can go to the doctor and not necessarily get that support. A lot falls on society and on charities to provide alternative solutions.

In some cases, if people come here it takes away the need for medication. Anti-depressants are often given when there are many other things that ultimately take longer and cost more but have a much longer-term view of the solution. Not placing blame on doctors but obviously it's easier for a doctor to write a prescription than to take someone along to an activity and keep track of how they get on and monitor the effect on their mental health.

Social prescribing started in Newcastle in about 2012 as a preventative tool and is spreading slowly to other areas. The organisation I work for is small and is predominantly for older people but because social services and mental health services are so stretched, they sometimes send us referrals for people who need complex support before they are ready to attend a group such as Flourish.

This makes things very difficult: you want people to succeed but, in terms of support, sometimes there are missing steps of the ladder that people need to climb in order to progress. It's a case of trying to do the best you can.

To make a good project like Flourish work, there has to be a leader who inspires a real sense of community, welcoming people that first time, bringing them into becoming part of something. I've taken people to some places and thought I wouldn't want to be part of it myself.

It's the people who make all the difference. You could have another gardening project in the same environment, right next door, and it might not work, just as two lunch clubs can have a very different atmosphere.

The staff at Flourish are amazing. I don't think they always see what they have created. You can't underestimate the value of community, or the challenge of creating it. People can tell if someone really cares or if they're just half-listening. This place is a lifeline for people. The combination of the outside environment and the work that goes on here is pretty special.

That's why I wanted to raise money for this place and it was worth all the effort. So many good projects fall down for lack of financial support. Flourish is a project that deserves to survive."

STORY 14: EMMA

As Pete and so many others have credited the staff with the success of their own or their client's or their loved one's increase in happiness, perhaps it's time to meet two of the project's key staff members.

Emma Browning is Flourish manager and Dr Anna Sweeney is the horticultural therapist and team leader. Professionally qualified, they have also both personally experienced the realities of mental health and its need to be nurtured, which may have enhanced the compassion and insight they bring to the project.

Emma begins:

"I did a degree in Art In A Social Context and as part of it I did art projects with people with mental health issues but it was really hard to get work in that field.

I had my own art practice of sculpture and installation but sitting at home being an artist Monday to Friday – that did not appeal!

So I decided to work in the social sector, without the art. I worked with homeless people, people with drug and alcohol addiction or HIV, in roles empowering, supporting and enabling people.

I had two children and my husband and I wanted to bring them up in the countryside. He retrained so we could move, changing from working in manufacturing to forestry, which was much more suited to him.

Because we moved with a young family and a big mortgage, I took the first job I could, at Bournemouth University as a diversity and equality advisor, but I wanted to be back in the charity sector.

I had been to Holton Lee a couple of times to see art exhibitions and eventually I left the university job to take up the role of volunteer co-ordinator here, in 2008. We got a big grant to support people living with disabilities to volunteer.

Holton Lee already had money to do horticultural therapy for people who could pay and at first we ran two separate projects, then we combined the two programmes because they naturally worked well together.

I have lived with a lifetime of mental and physical illness, from the age of 14. It may be a genetic thing; I'm not the only one in my family. I came from a loving family with a healthy upbringing, so there's no obvious cause.

So personally I have spent a long time getting a lot of help and learning to live well with a mental illness and I wanted to be able to pass some of it on to other people. Wherever people are, in their wellbeing, there are always things they can do to improve.

A lot of happiness is a choice, but we get stuck in negative patterns of thinking and don't realise we're doing it. So you can make a choice to think and act differently: from seeing everything as being wrong, you can be grateful for even tiny things in your life.

You can change how you see yourself: we all have things that are wrong with us but if you can love yourself warts and all, your life changes massively. And you can choose the people you surround yourself with and the activities you do that you love. If you used to love playing the guitar but it now sits in the cupboard and you're feeling depressed, take it out and start playing again. Sometimes you need to fake it at first, but then it starts to have an impact on your mood.

And as Gandhi said, 'The best way to find yourself is to lose yourself in the service of others.' If instead of thinking, 'Poor me,' and, 'I wish things were different,' you start being kind and caring to someone else, everything changes.

We need to find meaning and purpose; it doesn't need to be a big project or joining a big group, just something that gets you out of bed in the morning and that you can see makes a difference.

You need to value your strengths and to do the basics – eat well and exercise, in a way that suits you.

There are different 'interventions' in mental health: they may be interventions by medical experts – a doctor or counsellor or CBT (cognitive behavioural therapy) practitioner deciding a course of action or medication, which is often trial and error to find what suits the person.

But my favoured type of intervention is WRAP – a Wellbeing Recovery Action Plan. How it works is that when you are well, you write down all the things that contribute to your being well. That gives you a tool-kit: ring this friend, avoid that one, have a bath, go for a walk … Then when you are unwell, you take your own advice.

I used to volunteer for a breast-feeding clinic to support women with problems. One woman came in who was distressed, and the baby was distressed, because the baby wasn't feeding properly. She said she had had advice from her mother, the health visitor and the internet – all advising different things. I told her to trust her own instincts and think about what she wanted to do. She hadn't been given that option.

For Flourish, I wanted to give people a project that they could step into with anything going on in their life, and improve their wellbeing. It doesn't matter what your disability or your history is. If someone needs special support with a medical issue, we'll take that on board, but otherwise we're not really interested in what the specific problem is.

What I'm interested in learning is: what are the things you love to do; what do you find funny; what skills can you share with someone else; how willing are you to be helped?

For someone to get the most out of coming to Flourish, they need an open heart and an open mind. Some people have never been in a room with another disabled person so they need an open heart, to meet everybody. And you need an open mind to try something you may never have done before, like woodworking or gardening or crafts.

Someone who might find Flourish difficult would be someone very entrenched in their identity, convinced that they can't do something – or convinced that they can, when they can't yet! Or someone not willing to be helped or to share any of their life or their story. For mental health, you do need a bit of help at first to do things for yourself.

I've been working in this field for 18 years – I'm 45 now - so I know what one needs to do to be well, yet there are times in my life when I refuse to do those things. So why don't we do those things that we know keep us well? Why do we have the need to do things that keep us stuck in those negative patterns? I don't know!

Flourish is better than a stand-alone intervention like CBT, where you learn some skills for six weeks then go it alone. Coming here is subtler: you are living it and it rubs off on you longer-term.

If someone comes here three days a week and thinks about what they do on those days that makes them feel better, they can find things that make them feel good on the other days as well.

There have been some outstanding success stories. Steve, the site manager, is the most obvious. You wouldn't recognise him from the person he was six years ago.

And there was one man who was so isolated, he just lived with his mum and never went out. After four months we helped him get a volunteer position in a charity near his home and he became really integrated into his community. Two years later I got a letter asking for a reference for him because they wanted to employ him. I danced round the office!

Another big success was a lady who had had a nervous breakdown; all her relationships – family, partner and friends – had broken down. I had never seen anyone with such anxiety: she couldn't sit on a chair for even a few minutes and she was using alcohol to manage her emotions.

She had never been with a person with disabilities but within a few weeks we noticed how she was helping other people achieve their goals, and what a kind, funny, genuine person she was. She decided to volunteer at her local day centre and about six months after she started there, they offered her a job.

I remember writing a reference for that job, and eventually she got to see it and said, 'Thanks for making up that great reference for me.' She had a hard time believing I hadn't made anything up and she actually was that lovely a person.

It's fun working in the charity sector: you get the opportunity to be creative and try things out and you can see the results; you can see you are changing people's lives.

Of course there are stresses as well, like trying to get funding and spending so much time on administration, report writing and planning, dealing with the big picture. I still get satisfaction from this job as it is; you have to have somebody doing it. But I hate it if a day goes by and I haven't left my desk and gone down the garden.

If I won the lottery I would give up my job - and volunteer for Flourish in the garden!"

STORY 15: ANNA

Someone who spends most of her working day – and extra hours, early and late, as well – in the Flourish garden, is horticulturist Anna.

"It was through my own illness that my interest in social and therapeutic horticulture developed.

I didn't start out studying horticulture: I had worked as a teaching assistant, my MSc was in conservation and I had started a PhD, looking at the link between humans and the environment. During two months of fieldwork in Palestine I was looking at how a community's identity is affected by water, or the shortage of water. And I'd previously been in Uganda doing conservation work with groups, with people living close to a forest and close to chimpanzees!

Then in my mid-20s – I'm 35 now - I got very ill: I was walking into university one day and just couldn't take another step. It was brought on by a work ethic of working all day every day.

I experienced such distress every day that I would walk for hours and hours, just being outside. Then I asked my dad to build a raised bed to grow plants. I started with a few herbs and I found that just handling the plants and the earth really took me away from the feelings of distress. It allowed what's called 'attention restoration' – meaning you can be absorbed by the activity but it's not too demanding and it allows recovery from stress.

Recovery was a long process; I was two years out of employment. Then, through my parents going to a plant sale there, I found Cherry Tree Nursery, a charity offering therapeutic horticulture. I went and talked to Jess, the manager, and she suggested volunteering.

It was a loving, supportive, accepting place. Someone could go in and cry all day and it would be all right. You could just be you – didn't have to put a face on, and there was the shared experience of producing something.

From 2008 to 2010 I progressed from being a Cherry Tree volunteer to part-time work in the propagation unit, working with people, and I discovered I was good at talking to people and supporting them.

I started doing community outreach in schools, setting up little greenhouses and vegetable plots in containers, and trying out a few sensory exercises, like touching a tree blindfolded. It was introducing young people to nature but also talking a bit about mental health, telling them about people attending Cherry Tree sometimes being sad. The children still visit Cherry Tree now.

An organisation called Thrive runs short training courses and while I was at Cherry Tree I did one around mental health and therapeutic horticulture.

In 2010 I came to see Holton Lee and got talking to Karen, who was then the horticultural manager for the charity and had three-year Lottery funding to set up something similar to Cherry Tree. It would be a market garden to bring in people and to offer fresh produce to the local community.

It wasn't designed as a therapeutic venture but Karen got a lot of enquiries from parents of school-leavers who had been diagnosed with autism spectrum disorder and needed somewhere to move on to.

I started at Holton Lee as a volunteer one day a week, with young people with autism, then a member of staff gave me a form and said, 'Here you are, Anna, apply for this!' It was an offer from Vodafone to donate – not money but a person – to a project for a few months, working three days a week. So I was donated to Holton Lee! At the time I started, I was still managing depression and anxiety.

We called the project Growing Futures then after the funding for it ended, Emma started Flourish with an alternative model for people with any disability, which allowed for the diversity that we have today. The name Flourish came later.

We started with only five or six young people with autism or learning disabilities, and the focus was on growing vegetables for sale off-site. We had a few school groups coming in too, with their own staff.

Focus groups had shown us that there was a gap for people with disabilities engaging with meaningful work in their own communities, being part of decision-making and having choices: the kind of social inclusion that we take for granted.

When people are jointly engaged in something purposeful, it doesn't just have an effect on their own self-image and wellbeing: they start to really see each other and react to each other differently.

Aspects of this job are hard, trying to achieve a balance between sustainability and the person-centred, therapeutic nature of the project. It has to pay for itself; we have to make money to cover the costs. We had the Lottery grant funding for four years, which was incredible because it allowed us to maintain that focus on personal wellbeing. But then we re-applied for renewed funding and didn't get it.

Now money comes through the Livability central office fundraising team and through some of our donors, like Pete Thompson, who ran such incredible distances to raise money for mental health projects, including Flourish!

Anyone who wants to come to Flourish first comes on a taster day and if it works out for them we give them four months to come here free, then it's a paying service. Social Services fund some people through Direct Payments, but there are some who don't fit the categories. Sometimes they carry on here as volunteers for a while.

The idea is to support and improve an individual's wellbeing and, wherever possible, to help people move on. After two months, they have a review to see if they want to stay or to go and do something different. We're connected to a network of other projects.

One of them is the UCan project, which is now set up in the farmhouse. It works with the most vulnerable people who are unemployed and encourages some into the Flourish project. UCan has a lot of links with other organisations providing volunteering opportunities and work experience, which can lead to paid work.

Cherry Tree is an example of sheltered work. When someone is not allowed to go back into the work environment – or is forced back before they can manage - it can set them back years. Sensitive and understanding employment is what's needed – but I'm not sure it always exists!

Some people from Flourish have gone on to start their own gardening services or jobs within their own community, which is great. We want to support people to feel confident to be part of their local community and for that community to welcome them. Our first priority in Flourish is social interaction, using horticulture or other craft-based activities. Everyone who comes here has experienced some kind of isolation, whether it's from experiences of addiction or recovering from a stroke or other illness.

Because it's such a diverse group it's a challenge to meet each person's individual needs. But we take a strengths-based approach, starting with what the person is interested in and wants to do, which gives it meaning. And we try always to make it fun!

Sometimes there can be behavioural issues but we try to manage it through example: our values are about being open and kind to everyone. People do change their behaviour by seeing how others talk to each other and behave towards each other. Thankfully, we have never had to send anyone away!

We give people choices about what tasks they want to do that day but if someone comes in and refuses to do anything, encouragement doesn't really help; it's best to just let them be with the group, without actively joining in. Passive participation can be effective in certain situations. And as people start working together and laughing together, often the person will pick up a trowel and join in the work.

We start to learn what would benefit an individual who is having a bad day; for instance, physical activity helps some people – a task like wheeling a barrow to fetch loads of woodchip, without having to join in with other people. Or someone can take time to sit and just be - we have a quiet room and a quiet garden. Once someone starts relaxing, the resistance falls away.

The weather is obviously another challenge! With a diverse group, it can be hard trying to find things that everyone can do when the garden is 'resting' and it's cold and icy. But we do have an amazing team of bank-staff now with skills in arts and crafts, music and woodwork.

This year has been a difficult growing season, dry and hot, with seeds failing to germinate and some vegetables like lettuce tasting bitter because the soil was too hot. And of course if you run a growing project on organic principles, caring about the earth as well as the people, there are limitations on pest control and so there will be losses.

There are ways we can make things better, in the future. We have found that we are good at growing vegetable plants: at a recent plant sale we raised over £1,000! So we are now supplying a nursery. And we could also do a range of wildflower plants, as they grow so well in this environment.

But changing direction always requires money: for instance, we would require green polythene over the polytunnels instead of the clear polythene which lets in too much light for those plants, and we might need to relocate the polytunnels. And we really need another greenhouse! And more indoor space!

We are planning a Dutch barn, with part of it used to start a shop, selling produce but also woodwork items like wildlife homes. So we could do with more volunteers to prepare the items ready to be assembled so the work can be accessible to all.

And ideally we would have a café here, because that goes well with a farm shop and also with walkers and birdwatchers coming to the site; there is already a cottage here with downstairs space for one. But it all comes down to funding!

In terms of referrals, the project is well known now and we have a waiting list, though in terms of public awareness of the existence of this place and attracting customers, we still have some work to do.

I am very pleased with the way it's going, though – with the sense of community. That's what inspired me about Cherry Tree, and my dream here was to foster community.

I have had to learn to step back and focus on the people, when there are gardening disasters, like someone pulling up all the comfrey because they thought it was weeds, or somebody trampling the plants that have just been put in!

Perhaps because my training wasn't in horticulture, it hasn't been so hard to prioritise the people. We have learned to allow for losses – from bugs and climate and accidents – and just grow back-ups.

It has also helped that some of our outlets for vegetables are flexible: for instance, the Food Assembly, a local co-operative venture that allows buyers to source fresh produce online and collect it from a local hotel one day a week. Instead of putting 'cauliflowers available' on the page, I can put 'four cauliflowers' – and when they're gone, they're gone. And I supply a local health food shop that will just take whatever we have at the time, and we also make up veg boxes to order, from what we are harvesting. When we have the shop – hopefully! - we'll be able to do more.

I'm incredibly grateful for what I went through. That kind of experience gives you an empathy and a compassion you wouldn't have had otherwise; it's not theory. Cherry Tree, Growing Futures and Flourish, and my research in Palestine all helped me too, to recognise the universality of suffering but also the immense compassion and love that comes from this.

I met my husband at Holton Lee. He was volunteering in various projects like beekeeping and a vineyard at the time and through that he met a guy from Lush: the company had a demonstration garden here for teaching people about producing natural ingredients. So John came to have a look at Holton Lee and we got talking and realised we had that same interest in organic growing, beekeeping, etc. It has been wonderful how his role has grown, with his own workshop here and involvement in the Woodland Wellbeing project for people living with dementia, so he is not only working on the land but with the people.

We were engaged within six months and got married in 2015. We had the wedding party here at Holton Lee in a marquee on the back field and the staff and people from here came.

It was perfect, because we had met here and are a part of it."

STORY 16: VIABLE OUTCOMES

One of the buzzwords in healthcare is 'outcomes.' Any project or treatment has to be justified in measurable terms, to be considered worth continuing.

And it's easy to see progress in the stories of those who become physically fitter or socially more integrated or who gain skills. But what about people who will never become 'normal' or recover from their condition? What kind of positive outcome, if any, can be expected from their attendance at a project such as Flourish?

Sometimes parents or partners, in close daily contact with the person they lovingly care for, notice changes that are difficult to quantify and might well go unnoticed.

Small changes can seem miraculous in a person who is not expected to change, except for the worse.

A severely autistic young man accepts a slice of cake handed to him by someone who is not his carer. A young woman walks into the community room by herself, not clinging to her support worker. Someone laughs at a joke for the first time, or listens to a conversation and nods agreement, or looks someone in the eye instead of looking away.

Adrian is an example of someone whose medical condition is worsening but whose quality of life can still be enhanced.

Originally invited to take part in Flourish to give his wife some time off from coping with his dementia, Adrian has responded to being surrounded by nature and especially enjoys walking through the woods. He notices all the bird calls and is often able to identify them, and he points out small details that others may overlook, like a patch of foxgloves or even a beetle scurrying across the path.

He can identify models of planes or helicopters that fly overhead and other members of Flourish sometimes ask him what they are, and he likes to be asked about his career in the Merchant Navy. He can still initiate conversation and enjoys talking about rugby and about his grandchildren.

Although Adrian struggles with feeling disorientated and with judging distances, he is still able to do some mechanical tasks he was previously good at, such as sawing wood. He doesn't mind what he's asked to do and, as long as it's something he's capable of, he gets on with the job and gives it his best effort.

He relates well to small groups of people in a calm environment such as the Woodland Wellbeing group he now attends at Holton Lee and he remembers people though not their names. He looks forward to seeing a friend he refers to as 'the policeman' – who also lives with dementia and who always engages him in banter. The noise of the crowded community room makes Adrian agitated but individually he often laughs at the antics of some of the younger participants. He enjoys being teased by the volunteers and has not lost his sense of humour.

Adrian is held in affection by many of the group and can still show affection. After a recent session, when his wife came to pick him up, he exclaimed, 'There's my darling wife!' and the two did a slow-motion dance towards each other across the car park, both laughing.

Adrian's story is not happy-ever-after: his cognitive faculties are declining. But he is still Adrian and he knows he is loved.

Marcel, who is 89, is losing his memory but not his outgoing, sociable character. He says, "Flourish has got a very rewarding feel to it. I always feel it's going to be interesting. You meet such a wide selection of people, from all walks of life – even foreigners, like me! I'm half French. And when new people come, it's surprising how they develop the community.

"I used to have this clowning act and I made a lot of friends. Over the years a lot of children knew me as 'Uncle' and they became like family.

"I joined the army as a boy soldier during the war, then I had a job with a radio company but I lost it when the man who had been there before the war came out of the army and wanted his job back. So I went back into the army! I went to the military school of music at Twickenham. I played the French horn. Then when I was stationed in Germany, where they made wonderful musical instruments, I was able to buy my own – a German French horn!"

Marcel's daughter Noelle explains, "It was in Germany, while the soldiers were clearing out everything at the end of the war, that he came across a box of costumes, with several clown outfits, and he decided to use them for entertaining children – army children at first and then in the local community and in children's homes." Marcel ordered special oversized clown's shoes from the German shoemaking firm, Bata, and joined the national organisation for clowns. Noelle says, "He did a lot for charity – he was eventually awarded a British Empire Medal for it."

"I miss all the friends I made and the children I got to know over the years, through being a clown," Marcel adds. "So it's good to come here, to a place that feels like family again."

"At the end of the day, it's all about quality of living," Noelle says. "Coming to Flourish has been a real boost to his confidence. The team is so good, it doesn't matter if he doesn't remember things, and if there is any difficulty it's resolved quickly. For me, it's lovely meeting all the people here; it's good to see so many dedicated people helping. I have always been community-minded myself, and so has Marcel."

Robert is a young man with a difficult medical history, whose strength of personality only becomes apparent when people get to know him. He appeared shy when he first came to Flourish and stayed close to staff, and some of the other participants seemed unsure of how to relate to him because his verbal ability is limited. But in a film made about work in the Flourish garden Robert was shown watering seedlings - very thoroughly! When the film was shown to the group, everyone teased him about drowning the plants and he laughed along, and the ice was broken.

Robert is known for his one-word sentences that say everything he needs to say – especially, 'Why?' which he often uses to continue the conversation when someone is talking to him. Another favourite word is 'Work!' when he sees someone taking a break! He has made friends and everybody loves him. He comes out to welcome each person as they arrive in the morning and likes putting their photo up on the board in the community room. And he insists on being told what kind of cake a volunteer has brought in this week. His mother says he doesn't eat cake at home!

He comes to help at every event and volunteered to be the one to present a gift to Princess Anne when she visited Holton Lee. And although he tends to stand back and say, 'You!' when asked to do certain things (like weeding thistles or nettles) he has developed new capabilities such as photography. Recently when a volunteer was struggling to use a drill, Robert took it out of her hands and expertly fitted a new drill bit.

Recently his mother, Lorraine, came to work at Flourish. She talks about her son's life at home and at Holton Lee:

"Robert is the youngest of four boys. He had problems when he was born: he didn't have a sucking reflex so until the age of two and a half he had a nasal gastric tube, then he had a gastrostomy tube in the stomach.

"Till the age of five he had to be overnight fed because he couldn't take in enough food during the day. Even up to the age of ten he didn't eat a lot and I could never get him to take medicine. He only had the tube removed last year and he's 25 now.

"He went to a special school and loved it and everybody loved him, and he went to Poole College till he was 19.

"Robert was coming to Flourish before I knew anything about it! While he was at Poole College a group of them spent half a day a week here for six weeks. The first I knew was when I received a letter saying how much Robert was a valued part of Flourish.

"I was going to send him to another place but I saw he loved it here. He started on one day a week and I was going to increase it to two but then he went through a bout of anxiety so I kept him home.

"I didn't realise at the time how good they were here; I know now they would have made allowances for him and coped with it.

"So then he came back to Flourish for an hour, with me with him, but now he comes three days a week. If he had anxiety another time, I would send him. The staff here are really adaptable to the needs of the person.

"Robert goes to another group twice a week; they go out and about and it's good but he can get overlooked. At Flourish, if he's not joining in, someone will work with him one-to-one.

"He loves the people at Flourish and also enjoys whatever he does: birdwatching and gardening and using the wheelbarrow. He always asks me the day before if he is going to be coming tomorrow. Even in terrible thundery weather, he still wants to go!

"Flourish has benefited Robert's wellbeing a hundred percent. He's very relaxed and happy here and because he is, so am I! He's always been a friendly person but he has come out of himself more since he's been at Flourish; he really gets involved in everything he's doing.

"Even working here, I don't want to come on the same days as him because it's very much Robert's space. Flourish is Robert's happy place."

It's encouraging that Lorraine believes her son would come through a severe anxiety attack without having to be kept at home next time. Chris, another Flourish participant, recalls experiencing a breakdown during his time at Flourish:

"In 2015, I was here one day and I was really unwell; I had a massive breakdown. At four in the morning my mum phoned for an ambulance because I was in so much pain. But I got through it, thinking about this place and all the support behind me.

"I love it here. I love the atmosphere and I like working hard, working through a list of jobs, knowing I can get the job done and that it's worth doing the best I can. When I get home, I smile about it, thinking what I've done today.

"I don't have a favourite job; I like all of it – mechanics, shop work, wheelbarrowing manure and woodchip, shovelling, sowing seeds, harvesting, woodwork, making birdboxes.

"Having a mix of age groups is good because you can learn from older people what they know, and also you can show other people skills that they haven't learned yet and show new people what Holton Lee is about.

"I like working with other people and I've made so many friends that I don't know who to talk to first! It's easy to make friends here. I used to get bullied at school a lot and I didn't really know who to talk to. People can be hard on each other and don't listen. But here, I can tell people if I'm having a bad day and they'll listen to me."

Adam comments that Chris listens more and has become steadier in his time at Flourish and no longer runs off when the group is out for a walk. And staff say that Chris is now a lot more focused, more grounded and better at working in a team, and that he uses his imagination and creativity to bring happiness to other people, such as making birthday cards for them.

And what better outcome can there be than happiness?

STORY 17: HEALING THE UNSEEN WOUNDS

In the early days at Post Green, when Tom and Faith had just started a small Bible study group in their home, they invited an American evangelist they had only just met to stay with them. The evangelist, a lady called Jean Darnall, had – with the encouragement of her pastor husband Elmer who was away working in Hong Kong at the time – followed an inconveniently clear prompting from God to give up her home and all her possessions and to travel, with her teenage daughter, from one speaking engagement to another.

When Tom and Faith met her she was exhausted so with characteristic hospitality they invited her into their home to spend a few weeks recuperating.

Jean recovered quickly and began taking an interest in the Bible study group they had started. In her childhood, Jean had been healed of serious illness when someone prayed over her for God to heal her. Consequently, her faith in the power of God to intervene personally in a person's life, with miraculous results, was a major part of her ministry.

Physical and emotional healings began to be a regular part of the meetings at Post Green House, with the result that the small group soon grew to 300 attendees, which led to the development of the first Bible study camps in the paddock.

We will hear later about some examples of instant healing in response to prayer and faith. But in the meantime, having already met Christian, let's meet two women who have experienced healing through Flourish, in less dramatic ways but in the complex area of recovery from long-term emotional scars.

Jo and Caroline each tell their individual stories. Here's Jo first:

"I started at Flourish on a very cold January day. It's not far to drive but it was hard to get here, worrying about the car going wrong and whether I could get there for ten o'clock, even though I had been up since six. But I felt, 'Don't miss the opportunity.' When I came here, I had had three bereavements in ten months and had lived in unsafe accommodation. It felt really tough just trying to stay alive. I couldn't get through a day without crying and people naturally don't want to be around someone with problems but at Flourish it felt very inclusive, from the beginning.

I had been to other places for people with mental health issues but I hadn't got much out of it: in some places, staff were not trained or had compassion fatigue or tended to overlook things, and I worried about the other people.

For instance, someone might be judged as having problems with self-care and hygiene when no one had checked if they even had money for hot water and soap to get a wash in the morning. And while it's nice to go anywhere and chat and have friends, if it's all people with mental health issues, people can tend to dump on you. Coming here was like paradise: not that there was nothing to worry about but it felt safe to be here. I didn't worry about my own safety or the other people's and I didn't feel out of place or lacking. If you are able to ask, people will help you or they will know someone who can.

I don't find it easy to ask for help but it's one of the things I am learning, and it was nice to have choices of activity for the day and to have the chance to learn new things, and the facilities to do crafts.

If I have to ask how to do something, like change a drill bit in woodwork, I don't feel stupid. It's human nature to have a kind of hierarchy, according to what people can or can't do, but here it's different: it's a community.

In a community, you don't think about what a person has produced at the end of the day, but about everyone as a part of something whole, even if their part is a smile.

I had done gardening before; I didn't have a garden but I shared an allotment, so the allotment was my garden: it was like a wildlife sanctuary, with a bit of veg here and there.

In the last 20 years I have lost my home, because the landlord wanted to develop; I've had an accident and a head injury, then I moved into a house to share with a friend – that's when I had the allotment – but she was quite mentally ill herself. She said she was bipolar but later told me she had a serious personality disorder and also had malignant melanoma. I stayed in touch with her and helped her until she died, but for my own safety I had to move out. I was put in temporary accommodation. It was called a respite house but there was no supervision and I was sharing with strangers, one of whom trashed the place overnight. I didn't know who to phone. There was a list of numbers beside the pay phone but they were all out of use and no one answered.

I left messages at several places and in the morning someone sent the police round. The woman who was meant to be in charge was more concerned with getting the person to pay for damage to the property than with the safety of the residents.

Just a few months before my friend died, my mum had died and then my dad passed away – all in ten months. When I first came to Holton Lee to see around the place, I couldn't stop crying. It was a good thing there was a time delay before I started at Flourish because I needed time to grieve before I could be with people.

I would be totally isolated if I didn't come here: not that I wouldn't make the effort to go out, but nothing comes anywhere near what I get out of coming here.

I really enjoy making things out of wood and when I had been coming here a while and was making a lot of things, the staff offered me a space to have as my own workshop. I was overwhelmed. I still ask them every so often if it's really OK for me to have this and to keep using it whenever I want.

I used to do pottery and now I also help out in the clay workshop every week. I had the idea of making little ceramic bags by rolling the clay over hessian, so it picks up the imprint and looks like a sack. I thought this was something that people could make and that we could sell in the Flourish shop.

I've always been creative. I don't know if that's something in my parents' heritage, because I was adopted. I was brought up as one of five and I only learned later that one was my half-brother and the others weren't related to me at all.

I didn't find out till I was 21. My parents were away on holiday and my brother wanted his birth certificate so he went to the Registry Office and was told there was no one with his surname born on that day, though there was a boy with his Christian name. So he asked about the rest of us and found that I had the same mother as him but the father was unknown.

When my parents got back they had to admit it but the conversation was over and done with in ten minutes. My brother decided to go to the local paper with the story and I said, 'Don't include me,' but he did. My dad said it was just opening a can of worms – but it was my life, not worms!

With adult sight, I can see that my dad was suffering all his life from traumatic stress disorder from his time in the army and my mum loved babies but didn't know much about what to do with them after that stage.

The way it affected me was a complete loss of trust. At 21, I lost my identity. I felt I had gone through all my childhood for nothing. You are hard-wired to stay in your family unit and be loyal to it because that's your only chance of survival, so you just live with the way things are. You may become a victim of that or some people may become criminal and angry. I'm now in my 50s and still don't really know what I have become yet.

Coming here is like a moment in space and time – not just a breathing space but an oxygen tent! I've learned to try and speak a bit more about myself. Before, I wouldn't do that because of trust issues.

Over the years I've had people from various social services come into my life but I did find it difficult to trust them. One time, I had an appointment at my house but the person didn't turn up – but she put down on the record that I forgot about it. So it made me wonder what people were writing about me.

Another time I was given a formal letter of eviction because I was told it would push me up the housing list but then I was told I had to accept whatever I was offered because 'beggars can't be choosers.' It's a bit last-century, that! I wasn't a beggar.

Nowadays, even bank managers will say, 'Come in and talk to us if you have mental health issues,' but they don't necessarily understand what the issues are, and of course they're not allowed to include people who might be disruptive or detrimental.

Society's view of mental illness tends to be weakness, laziness or a threat. It all comes under the same heading, whether someone's condition causes mild confusion or behaviour that could be dangerous.

Sometimes I tell myself, 'You can only give up once,' therefore you need to think about what it is you really want to give up. It might not be myself that I want to give up. One end of the scale might be looking hard at that urge to self-harm, and at the other end of the scale is allowing yourself to experience joy, or even recognising that feeling.

Coming here has really helped me. It's not a question of going at my own pace – I don't have a pace. It's hard to get myself going. But last year, I came in at weekends and did the watering, though I worried a lot about the responsibility in case plants died or I missed something.

This year I've done the watering again but it hasn't worried me. This summer, by 8.30am it was really hot and watering the beds and polytunnels and greenhouse can take three hours, but I would get here at six in the morning and go home after the rush hour traffic. For three nights I actually slept here in a little tent and it was really nice. I still felt safe."

Caroline is also someone who lost her home, her beloved allotment and her health, as well as struggling with marriage and some difficult relationships. With little hope that things would improve, she found that over time her outlook on life became much more positive. Her story is a testimony to the need for any real healing to be social, as well as physical and emotional.

"I had a stroke in 2017. I was extremely lucky: apart from tingling in my left arm and leg, and peripheral vision in my left eye, I've recovered and lived to tell the tale.

But I had to give up my allotment, which I loved; I also had lung cancer, in 2014, and had the upper left lobe of my lung removed. And I was diagnosed with osteoporosis in the spine. I thought, 'What else is going to happen to me?' I got very frustrated.

When a lady from the local social prescribing agency introduced me to Holton Lee, I was surprised: how many times had I driven past this place and never realised it was there! I was in awe when I saw it: what a fabulous place to be!

It was the best thing that happened to me: I live on my own and it's very nice to come out and meet other people, and we all love the garden.

Everything here is geared up for helping people in every situation, in wheelchairs or whatever. You don't always know what kind of disability people have. I don't consider myself disabled but I do struggle a bit when we go on walks. I can use the buggies but I want to do more walking.

The first time I came out here, my job was weeding and I hate weeding! But it didn't put me off. I love it out here. I love the people and the things that we do – though sometimes I think, 'Not *more* potting on!'

Although I had previous experience of gardening, with the allotment, I like the fact that I am still learning, like the correct way to prune apple trees.

I was born in Scotland and we moved down south in 1962, when I was 11. My mother and her partner bought a bungalow near where I live now, so I've almost come back to my roots.

I did quite well at school; I was very sporty and wanted to become a PE teacher but my exam results weren't good enough and there was no careers advisor to tell you where to apply. It was suggested that I could become an occupational therapist but that didn't materialise either, so I just went and got a driving job, then later a job in a jewellers', where I met my husband. I was 18 when I got engaged. We married in 1973.

We decided we were going to get into the pub trade and went as trainee managers, living in and learning all aspects of the hospitality business. The owners had an African grey parrot called Wilfred: people used to come in just to see him! They also had a dog called Winston and the parrot used to wind him up by using the owner's voice!

But the job was very long hours for very little pay and I got quite down, so we moved back with my mother. My husband Andrew was working night shifts then he decided to become a construction worker, which was better money.

Through a co-ownership scheme we got a flat next door to another pub and I started working there, at first doing cleaning then bar work. I was there for quite a few years and formed a ladies' darts team, going around to different pubs, which was fun.

A friend who worked in the bar and lived in the same flats also did cleaning jobs and when she had too many she asked me to help out, so we went into business together. I didn't have money to invest so my contribution was to work a number of hours for free.

The business grew and we ended up with 12 cleaners working for us. I was there for two or three years then I lost my driving licence through drink-driving and couldn't get to my clients any more. This friend's father was area manager for a pub franchise so Andrew and I decided to go back to the pub trade. But running your own pub is hard and Andrew got threatened, which made me very jittery. There was just one family that caused trouble but I used to walk to the bank, carrying the money, and it felt unsafe. So we moved back to Dorset and I went back to working at the same pub, then another one where we used to drink, first cleaning and then working behind the bar.

I am still friends with the owner, Annie. Her husband was a very keen gardener and when he died in 1993, I offered to cut the grass and the hedge for her while she kept on with flowers, which had won Best Pub Frontage for two years in a row. Annie taught me how to deadhead roses. That's how I got into gardening!

My mother had got into financial difficulties so we sold our co-owned flat and bought the bungalow from her. She died in 1989 and my sister, who is 14 years older than me and lives in South Africa, invited us out to Durban for three months, which was lovely. Andrew wanted to move out there and we did look into it but it wasn't practicable.

I've never been out of work but Andrew was always flitting from job to job and that was a strain. We couldn't keep up the payments on the bungalow and it was repossessed, and we moved into rented accommodation.

In 1998 I went to work as a cleaning supervisor. The cleaning work was outsourced to an agency but I helped draft the contract and monitored the standard of cleaning and I used to go to conferences with my line manager. I was there for 16 years until I retired.

Andrew went back to college to get his BTech in construction and progressed to being a site manager, and we got a mortgage and bought an old Victorian house. All the floors sloped and it needed wall ties and was damp.

In 2002, I left him. I am gay: I've always known it, and I met a woman and fell head over heels in love. That had never happened before. I don't think Andrew was entirely surprised that I was gay but he didn't think I would leave, so that was a shock.

I had got married because it was the norm: you got married and had children; it was expected. We never had children and didn't pursue it, just thought if it happens, it happens.

The woman had a long-term girlfriend at the time but we moved in together, into rented accommodation. Then we managed to get a mortgage and jointly bought a house. But sharing a kitchen led to terrible fights, always over stupid little things, that eventually split us up and she moved out.

But she has always been supportive; if there are repairs needed on the house she always pays half, and we're still friends. She was the first person I phoned when I had the stroke. She wasn't home but her partner called her and she knew as soon as she saw me that I'd had a stroke because her father had had one.

I miss going to work. I would have kept working if I could. When I worked, life had a structure to it. But since I got extra funding, I now come to Flourish two days a week. I met a former customer from the pub here recently, so that was a link with the past!

And I just love being part of this place. It always helps my mood; I can't wait to get here. It's a community: regardless of disabilities, we all connect and work together as a team.

We were coming back from a walk one afternoon and I said, 'I just love this place!' and one of the staff members said, 'We love you!' What more can you ask?"

STORY 18: SOMETHING MORE?

"What more can you ask?" is a question that draws many responses. It's natural for human beings to want more – to reach for the best, the utmost, for themselves and for others.

Being grateful for everything we have sounds more likeable than always wanting more – but if more could be possible, it would be a waste to keep a closed mind to it.

It's clear from all these accounts that something good is going on in this place, something that the originators would probably be more than happy to witness, but it still begs the question … is there more?

Healing – both gradual and dramatically instant healing – was such a part of the life of the Post Green Community. And so many people experienced a sense of peace that was overwhelming, different from anything they had felt before and at a depth that changed the course of their lives.

So – what was it, that 'something more?'

Someone who found herself wanting more was Lois, whose experience years ago at Post Green opened her eyes – and ears! – to a dimension of life she hadn't been offered before.

"I was brought up in a household where both parents were anti-church. At school I got a grounding in the Bible, and in the Girl Guides we had to go to church parade but I found the services very boring. But at teacher training college in Weymouth I met Christians whose lives seemed different from others' and as a result of their witness I became a Christian in 1971.

In 1972, one of them hired a minibus to take students to a Saturday evening conference at Post Green and I went along. We arrived late; the meeting had already started. From outside I heard the most beautiful music – the sound and the harmony were really 'out of this world' - but when we went in I couldn't see any choir or loudspeakers and I couldn't see how it was all happening. Then one of my friends whispered, 'They're singing in tongues – I meant to tell you about that!'

It awakened something in me and I wanted more.

I attended two May Bank Holiday camps at Post Green, one while I was at college and one the year after I left, held in the orchard at the back of the house, before the camps moved to Holton Lee.

I don't know what it was about the atmosphere there that was different from the churches I had been to. One thing – it sounds such a small, silly thing but it made an impression on me – was that although we were camping and there were the usual Elsan chemical toilets behind a canvas screen, we were allowed into the house to use the toilet in their home! And I remember that their kitchen always seemed to be crowded with people.

At the camp, I asked for prayer to receive the Holy Spirit and I had the experience of being flooded with peace.

How can I sum up what it was like at Post Green? It was like a fountain of living water in a dry and arid land. It quenched one's spiritual thirst in a way that wasn't offered by most churches at that time. It was a feast - not just basic bread but cake as well!

That experience at Post Green and the camps I attended there gave me a foundation that has kept me strong throughout my life, through all the storms. It had a very strong impact on my life. Being at Post Green was an experience of being loved, and that's what drew people in."

Experiencing being loved is certainly something that is still happening today at Holton Lee, and still drawing people in. Flourish has recently had to expand to four days a week from three, and there is a waiting list.

But, like Lois, some of the people who experienced the 'gifts of the Spirit' like praying and singing in tongues, hearing or feeling unmistakable promptings from God, and praying for humanly impossible healings, seem very sure that human love is only the pre-condition for God to intervene in the lives of ordinary people, with some extraordinary outcomes.

So let's meet a few people who have had those life-changing experiences, some of whom were initially cynical, or wary of 'weird and wonderful' things, and yet somehow had a feeling that there might be something more ...

Not all miracles are universally welcome. One man who had been badly injured in a car accident attended a healing service at a local church where he saw people get out of their wheelchairs and walk. His response was, "I'm not losing all my benefits and going back to work!" and he left abruptly.

And maybe not all sicknesses and injuries need the same kind of obvious healing. Some symptoms may be the body's kindly warning to slow down, to change our lifestyle or reassess our priorities. It's unwelcome but needed.

Sickness can turn someone's life upside down, but so can healing - and that's when it's free and genuine. How about all the money-making scams exploiting people's emotions by claiming to cure every condition, confer prosperity or change lives? No wonder people are wary.

While churches should be accessible doorways to God's love, forgiveness and grace, as organisations they are as open to flaws as any institution on earth, because they are full of imperfect human beings. So the best that anyone can do, if they're looking for more love and goodness, is to go cautiously, listen to people they already trust, and listen most of all to their gut instincts.

That's what Bob, the father of a former Flourish volunteer, did in 2003. Naturally sceptical and a lifelong atheist, he began, in response to a young grandson's concern for him, to question his own attitudes.

His is a back-to-front story of healing – faith first then sickness - that shocked as many Christians as it challenged fellow atheists!

"I would describe myself as a cynical Yorkshireman. With hindsight I would say that for years God was standing outside my life, knocking at the door, but for 75 of those years I dismissed the concept of God.

I couldn't dismiss the concepts of life and death so easily, having a fascination with nature and a series of close shaves with death! I was born in 1927 and I survived a near bomb-blast, a couple of potentially fatal accidents while working on the railways and laying gas pipes, and being attacked with a cut-throat razor in a fight. That's when for the first time I thought about death. I imagined it like a deep sleep but with no awakening.

I didn't have faith in God but I respected people who had; the Christians I met had a kind of inner peace. But it was something I couldn't make myself believe in.

When I met my wife, she and her two sons - who are both ministers now - and all her family and friends were Christians. No one ever pressured me. They and a lot of other people were praying for me over the years, to come to God, but I never knew it.

I'd take my wife to church sometimes but I wouldn't go in. It wasn't for me. I'd have felt uncomfortable, and I didn't want to pretend.

The only thing that made me think was my nine-year old grandson. He was worried about me, that I wouldn't be in heaven with him, and he asked me why I didn't believe in God.

I said that not everyone believes, and he said would I think about it? So I said yes, I would. And having promised, I kept my word and I did think - about why I was uncomfortable with belief in God, why I had put up a barrier, and why I am alive.

It was just wanting to know a bit more that made me go along to an Alpha course. I didn't want to join the church or anything; I just wanted to know what was putting me off.

They showed us a video the first night and some of the things that were said about Christ made me think. I knew some of the story, about God coming down as Jesus, and Jesus being crucified. I found it strange hearing about miracles but I saw it wasn't impossible. If he is God, and creator of the universe, then all things are possible.

But the evening ended with a prayer and I was uncomfortable with that. I felt like a hypocrite, being there, and I thought I wouldn't go back. But the second week was going to be a discussion so I gave it a chance, and the questions and answers were interesting. I decided I would finish the course; otherwise it would be pointless.

I asked a lot of questions and I still do. But I saw it was all right to have doubts and wonder about things. I had trouble believing in the existence of the devil. Then I saw that if you believe in God, who is good, you have to believe in the opposite.

The Alpha course included an away-day. I was struggling with the idea of being filled with the Holy Spirit and being forgiven for sinfulness: I didn't know if that was possible really.

When the speaker started on about talking in tongues and laying on of hands for receiving the Holy Spirit, I ran away – I knocked over a chair on my way out, I was in such a hurry!

I stayed outside till they were finished. It was a lovely autumn day, blue sky, with these two silver birch trees – picturesque - and I felt at peace. Suddenly a lot of leaves started to fall off one of the trees, in a shower, very slowly – and there was no wind.

About thirty seconds later, the other tree shed a lot of its leaves in the same way, and I was still looking around to see where the wind was coming from. There was no wind at all. It was beautiful, all the leaves raining down like that.

Two girls came outside and I asked them if the praying was over and they said yes, and people had received the Holy Spirit and they all showed different signs. It was only afterwards that it came to me that this had been my sign – all those leaves! So I hadn't escaped the Holy Spirit after all!

The minister started having one-to-one meetings with me and realised I still had this stumbling block about forgiveness of sins. He told me, 'Before you come next week, write down all your sins on a piece of paper and bring it with you,' and I said, 'The paper won't be long enough!'

When I was writing the list, I thought of things I'd said and done and I was trying to leave some out, then I thought - who was I fooling? God knows it all. But when I saw it all there in print, it shocked me; I felt ashamed.

I gave the minister my list of sins and he read it.

What he did then, I'll never forget. He held up the paper and set fire to it, from the bottom. I could see the flame gradually eating its way up the page, line by line, all the words disappearing, till it was ashes. It makes me cry even now, to think of it.

It's not hard now to ask forgiveness from God. If you try to turn away from sin, he'll help you.

I got baptized on June 1st 2003. Shortly afterwards my wife and I were out for a meal with the family and I had trouble swallowing. An endoscopy confirmed I had cancer of the oesophagus and I started treatment.

I thought whatever happened it was God's will. I tried to think what it would have been like to cope with this if I didn't have a faith, and I couldn't remember what it felt like not to have faith! I felt at peace with my life, and that it was in the hands of God.

Not all my fellow Christians shared that assurance. People were shaken, that the illness came so soon after my baptism, but because of the timing I was on a cloud of prayer just when I needed it.

My worst moment was when I saw myself in the mirror getting out of the bath in the hospital. I knew I'd lost weight – I'd gone from 12 stone to eight and a half – but I looked like something out of Belsen. That shook me.

The cancer was incurable because it was practically the full length of the gullet. Others who were with me in the hospice all died within two months, and the same was expected of me. But five years later I'd put weight on – a bit too much really! And I was walking without a stick.

I was going to the hospice once a week and when that stopped I wanted to keep going as a volunteer, talking to the patients, but that's not allowed so God must have something else for me to do. I've helped out a bit on the Alpha course.

They'll never say I'm cured, and I was warned that things could get bad again. But for now I live for the day. I spent a week away at a Christian festival and I found myself with my hands in the air, during the praise. Me!

It's sixteen years ago now. I have a few problems with swallowing, because of the scar tissue, and sometimes I wish that God would use me more.

But I think my story has encouraged a few people, as it encouraged me when people prayed for me when I was ill. I'm in God's hands, and I'm still here, breathing and walking around, so I've got nothing to complain about. I'm a few months off 92 and hoping to make it to my birthday, anyway!"

STORY 19: WHEELCHAIR TO WALKING

Bob would say that the change in his attitude was the real miracle, before and during the illness and regardless of his physical healing. Simon, healed of paralysis at Post Green at the age of 35, has a slightly different story. He had no prospect of ever walking again or being free from pain and was resigned to spending the rest of his life as a wheelchair user. His GP recorded the cause of his sudden recovery as 'a Christian experience' and a specialist described his case as 'extremely unusual.'

Simon recalls, "When I was eight I started suffering back pain but I just thought everyone had trouble getting to sleep because their back hurt."

It was in his early twenties, volunteering with the Mission to Seamen, that he woke up one morning in such pain he couldn't move. Test results were inconclusive and he continued working and received treatment from a chiropractor. But in 1981 he was hospitalised for slipped discs, followed by a second operation the following year, which left him with painful scar tissue, a collapsed vertebra, a bone graft, a hole in his spine and a spinal fluid leak that required further surgery.

Working on a river ferry, Simon's back gave way again and another operation left him in so much pain that he says, "I could only walk with a shuffle." It wasn't all bad news, as forced to take a job in a pub instead of working his boat, he met his future wife Julia and the couple now have two grown-up children.

Short of income, the couple took temporary jobs and lived in a bedsit, till Simon secured a job selling double glazing and they moved to Dorset, where they attended a local church and got married after two years. But shortly after moving house again, Simon was admitted to hospital with severe head and back pains caused by another spinal fluid leak. Surgery improved his walking but left him with painful sciatica.

It was hard to find employment but after six months driving HGV lorries, he trained as a driving instructor and took over a driving school from a man who was retiring.

"I was soon earning enough to keep Julia, our two children and a dog alive – but one day I woke up with this incredible pain in my lower back. I had to cancel all my driving lessons, phone around the local driving schools and pass all my pupils on to them.

So in May 1991 I was admitted to hospital again, with loss of sensation in my right leg and no reflexes in either leg. I lay in bed for 11 weeks and was told in July that I would never walk again. I did leave hospital with one leg working but I was in an enormous amount of pain. Julia was left to fend for the two children and for myself; I was in too much pain even to wash or dress myself. The driving school collapsed, my instructor's licence was revoked and my HGV licence ran out."

The impact on their lives was severe but the couple managed to stay fairly positive, Simon says. "But then I was admitted to hospital again, where the other leg stopped working. The doctors found scarring in the spine and also some hereditary disease that caused lumps to grow on the growing plates of the vertebrae, which explained much of the pain."

The doctors didn't expect Simon ever to be able to walk again or be free from pain and the family had to adjust to living with his permanent disability and struggling to obtain the necessary support from social services.

"We eventually got a ramp to the front door and a stair lift, and plans were being drawn up to adapt the house with an extension. In the meantime, a new church and community centre had been built and as it was only two minutes' wheel from our house we decided to give it a go. After only a few weeks I was asked if I would be interested in joining a worship group that was being formed and I agreed, singing with the group and putting on little skits.

In the autumn of 1992 I was asked if I would be interested in singing at a Christian camp. I agreed but worried about what I was letting myself in for – what brainwashing techniques would I be subjected to at this Post Green Camp, and who were these 'community' weirdos?

By the time I arrived at the camp I was in agony and I honestly thought I would be going home long before the end. I spent two nights sleeping on a bed in Holton farmhouse, waking up at two in the morning in such pain that I was crying out and desperate for painkillers.

But even with the painful nights, I was enjoying myself, singing on stage with the worship group at all the services. And my fears about the camp and the Community proved totally unfounded!

On the Saturday evening the main marquee was filled with this real sense of the presence of God. Then the singer standing to the right of me started to talk in tongues. I had never heard anything like this before and tried to listen to see if I could understand anything. It sounded sort of Arabic.

I was suddenly, without warning, filled with an incredible feeling of love, happiness and a tingling, which I later realised was the Holy Spirit coming into me. I was happy – I was ecstatic – and with that happiness I cried. I stopped singing and cried with joy. This for me was something out of the ordinary, especially in front of 500 people.

One of the leaders of the weekend came up and prayed with me. He started to cry too. Then our crying turned to giggles and finally to open laughter.

The songs I was singing suddenly meant something, my life meant so much more, and I just knew that if I did something – but I didn't know what – I would walk again.

Afterwards I was elated and very emotional. I was aware of this strong thought, which said, "I love YOU." Incredibly, I then realised I was free of pain, even the pain I had had since I was very young.

The painkillers I was on were one step away from opiates and therefore addictive so I didn't stop them immediately but weaned myself off them.

After the experience with the Holy Spirit I had two dreams, in both of which I saw myself get up and stand and then walk away from the wheelchair. But there was something I had to do first. And what was it? I didn't know.

The following Friday, I was talking to someone from our church and he was telling me of the healing he had received and of his experiences talking with God. This helped me a great deal when I woke up the following morning at about three a.m and God spoke to me, clearly and concisely: 'Just tell Julia what happened to you last Saturday and you'll walk away from your chair and never need it for this reason again.'

Clear and straightforward. None of the Thees and Thous I had expected! But I lay awake worrying about the consequences of telling Julia. She was a scientist and her beliefs were a bit shaky. We were halfway through getting an extension from Social Services – what would happen to that and what would we live on when we came off benefits? And would I be making a total fool of myself and nothing would happen at all?

Before I went downstairs for breakfast, I wheeled myself into the bathroom and tried my hardest to move my legs, without success. Then I went downstairs.

I started, 'Julia, I have something that I have to tell you about last weekend …' then I dried up. Finally I blurted out, 'Last weekend I had this amazing experience …'

Ten seconds after I finished telling Julia, I felt this rushing feeling of life flowing down my legs. They suddenly felt strong again. The nerves, which ten seconds ago had been struggling even to notice the children climbing up them, suddenly woke up. I could feel my socks and shoes.

I sat there full of hope, but not daring to try my legs out.

'Go on then, move them,' Julia said.

I summoned all my strength as I thought that even if they did work it would only be a slight movement that would grow stronger as I used them. But I kicked the wheelchair foot-rest out of the way with an incredible force, and we both burst out crying.

I then thought that if it was as easy as that, the other leg might move as well. So I tried, with more caution, and it was so easy. No stiffness or the pain I was expecting.

Within two minutes I was standing doing the washing up and putting things away on shelves I hadn't been able to reach for the past two years.

That day I was singing again, with the worship group at Post Green's 25th anniversary. I spent the day in the wheelchair, which was very difficult. It wasn't that I didn't believe it had happened but I just needed time for it to sink in.

But now I'm happy to talk about it to anyone who wants to listen. God has shown me his power and his love. Now he wants me to go out and spread the story of the miracle of my healing. I have been free of pain and sciatica and able to walk unaided since Saturday 5 June, 1992."

STORY 20: MIRACLES, MIRTH AND MANURE

Even where there is a sudden visible change in someone's life, a miracle is never instant. There will have been a long time of gradual unseen preparation before the change, and there needs to be a commitment afterwards to keeping the miracle alive by embracing a changed attitude and new life.

People who have experienced a miraculous personal healing may also be put under pressure from other people to be always jubilant and successful, when like anyone else they will go on to experience all kinds of other challenges and tragedies in their life and may struggle at times to keep their faith fresh.

Some miracles may appear major and others minor but common factors seem to be that they all require an openness to possibilities and they go beyond the confines of human achievement. And they are frequently accompanied by unconfined outbursts of joy!

The recent oral history project on Holton Lee has highlighted the physical transformation of the site itself.

Anyone who works in the Flourish garden comments on the quality of the soil, enriched season after season with manure from the stables nearby and bulked up with woodchip from a local tree surgeon.

And customers remark on the health of the vegetables, fruit and garden plants, all grown by organic methods.

But this transformation of poor sandy soil to rich soil full of essential nutrients is no overnight success. It results from the real miracle of a long history of people with vision to see the potential of the site and the commitment and skills to develop it.

An example of an everyday Flourish miracle is the construction of a new pumpkin bed. Running out of soil space for all the young pumpkin and squash plants bursting out of their nursery pots, the horticulture staff proposed using permaculture methods to build up a bank of fertile growing medium on a grassy area, without digging it all up first.

The whole group that day, including some youngsters with severe disabilities who had only just started attending the project, and a support worker on his very first day of work there, shared the task. First, donated sheets of cardboard from used packing boxes were laid over the ground to form a weed-proof barrier. This involved fetching the sheets from one of the polytunnels and carrying them to the site.

This sounds a simple task, but had to take into account the fact that some participants found it upsetting to walk into an unknown area or to have other people around them in a confined space. Others had to be shown that carrying a large sheet of rigid cardboard requires making a detour around someone coming in the other direction, who could be knocked over by it.

New skills were absorbed and aversions overcome. A young woman who was afraid to touch things or to be touched by anything agreed to share the carrying of a piece of board with another person, as long as she didn't have to go near the manure. Then the cardboard sheets had to be laid on the patch of grass designated for the bed, not elsewhere, and side by side, slightly overlapping, not on top of one another or far apart. For people with a brain injury or altered perception, this required spatial awareness that didn't come automatically.

Then those with physical strength wheeled barrows to and from the manure pile, while those with good co-ordination as well as physical strength shovelled manure into those barrows, which had to be held still during the process.

Care had to be taken that the barrows were unloaded on to the area of cardboard and not somewhere else. One care worker, momentarily distracted by the noise of jackdaws in the tall trees, received an unforeseen gift of manure over his boots and legs.

A few of the newcomers enjoyed the experience of walking and jumping on the spongy texture of the manure and had to be encouraged to return to the grass. A lad who liked things to be done in a proper manner became agitated at the mess caused by this behaviour and had to be reassured that the end result would be positive.

The next stage was to cover the manure with absorbent dry materials – torn-up newspapers and egg-boxes. The skills to tear them had to be demonstrated to the newer participants, and proved difficult for some to master.

Boxes that were flung intact on to the large heap were rescued by more experienced Flourishers wading into the manure and ripping them up before redistributing them. Everyone's boots acquired thick soles of manure, weighting the wearers down and making their movements ponderous, like astronauts.

Meanwhile, a strong wind had sprung up and sudden gusts whipped off people's hats and hoods and sent sheets of tabloid gossip whirling into the air, into the trees, the raspberry canes and the nearby community allotments. The group dispersed, chasing escaped items here, there and everywhere.

It was decided to water the newspaper layer as soon as it was laid down, to prevent it from blowing away. The hose was unravelled, the allotment tap wrestled with, and watering cans were filled from the nearest storage tanks. People flung cans of water or poured it all on to the same small patch, or failed to dodge the trajectory of the hose. There was movement, confusion, wet clothes and infectious laughter.

The new support worker said it was not quite what he had expected when he got up for work this morning but it had proved much more enjoyable!

When the bed was finished and ready for the next day's group to plant out, everyone stood round the newly-made bank and clapped. Those who found standing difficult sat on tree stumps or on chairs fetched from the polytunnel as everyone applauded the morning's work.

On the way back to the toolshed, people teased one another about their dishevelled appearance and raced each other with wheelbarrows.

The community room, at coffee break, smelt of manure and contentment.

If you're going to create a new garden, and work a few minor miracles along the way, that's not a bad way to do it.

STORY 21: THE PLACE OF FAITH

When work such as takes place at Holton Lee is so effective and fruitful, the question could be asked: "Why is there any need to bring God into it?"

But another question may be: "When it's so good, isn't he there already? And why would anyone want to keep him out?"

The work at Holton Lee could not be done without faith. It takes faith to remain mindful of the miracles, major and minor, that occur daily, weekly, hourly or over years and to celebrate them even on the difficult days.

A young man with autism, locked into a private world, after many sessions at Flourish over more than a year, one day looked at someone rather than past them.

He walked into a room and sat down, without having to be told where to go. He stopped flinching when anyone spoke to him or sat next to him. He accepted a cup of tea from somebody's hand. He attended the Christmas party and, when there was too much activity around him, he didn't run out or lash out but found himself a space to jump around until he felt calm.

A girl who was afraid to walk on different surfaces now walks from the community room to the garden, from hard paths to soft grass, from woodchip surfaces to compacted soil. She doesn't scream or push people away when they put something on the table in front of her. She stands up and looks at posters on the wall instead of sitting with her head tucked into her chest. She communicates that she enjoys certain tasks.

A man with a long history of depression gets up in the morning, gets dressed, has breakfast, and waits for transport. He walks into the community room, makes coffee, asks the person next to him if they want one, and discusses something he heard on the news. He chooses an option from the list of the day's activities and joins a group in the workshop making bird tables for sale. He eats lunch with people and chats with them, and goes home feeling the day has not been wasted.

For the staff and volunteers, it's encouraging to see these small – and hugely significant – signs of progress. But their engagement with each person's individual story also causes inevitable sadness if that person gives up coming or takes a downward turn in their health.

It takes faith to renew that same hope for the next person who is referred, or refers themselves, to the project, to see potential in them and work with them to find the best way to develop it.

Faith has very little to do with certainty or fixed beliefs – in fact, faith requires honest doubt and questioning, the humility to be proved wrong and a willingness to learn from mistakes.

It involves recognising that our human limits can never meet the whole depth of human need, giving up our requirement for perfection or self-sufficiency or the pressure to drive ourselves to exhaustion, and having the grace to leave gaps.

Probably we have all heard of social projects, or clubs or churches or businesses, that begin with good-hearted motives but over time turn sour. Often the leaders try to fix the conflicts by reorganising or planning new strategies or employing costly consultants, when the seed of decline is something imperceptible - a tiny and subtle shift in the spirit, a dissonance in the way that people view or assess one another, an attitude that might be described as an invisible sneer. Without a stronger spirit to override it, it can spread throughout a community or company and spell the death of it.

Holton Lee arose from a Christian community and is now part of Livability, a Christian charity, but it doesn't exist only for Christians or judge its employees on any standard except their personal ability and integrity.

It's a well-known theory that only Christ knows who the Christians are. It's not a label that people can claim or disclaim for themselves. If you go where the love is, sooner or later in some way you become aware of God. And a commitment to being human in the best and most truthful way possible is a look in the same direction as Jesus Christ.

I used to think that marriage was not for me, till my sister pointed out that I was looking at other people's marriages and thinking, "That's not for me!" Similarly, looking as an outsider at another person's faith might well put me off engaging with God at all. But the relationship can only be personal and individual, not a clone of someone else's.

It's not offensive to suggest that, even with the best project, there may be an indefinable 'something more' to be had: it is what the most dedicated leaders want – whatever achieves the best for everyone involved. And it's the opposite of being a demand for already hard-working people to do better than their best; it's more of a response to grace, allowing God to shoulder more of the load. Without faith, it is perfectly possible to run projects, do useful work and provide facilities for people. There's no shortage of projects for all kinds of good causes.

But it's not possible, without faith, to foster and nurture a living community of people who feel accepted and valued and empowered to accept and value others.

The ability to persevere faithfully with a personal depth of vision and commitment despite difficulties, disappointments and just not knowing what tomorrow holds, without breaking down under the weight of responsibility, is what faith offers.

God is faithful. If we can only keep faithfully trusting and moving forward, then it's a partnership that can't fail, whether you are living with disabilities or struggling with personal challenges or trying to support somebody who's finding life difficult.

Simple.

Though never easy!

If you have enjoyed this book, would you consider buying a copy for a friend?

Available from Amazon.

All profits and donations will go to the Flourish project, Livability Holton Lee, to continue its work.

Other books by Clare Nonhebel:

Fiction

Cold Showers *(winner of a Betty Trask Award for fiction)*

The Partisan

Incentives

Child's Play

Eldred Jones

Popcorn *(a novella)*

The Healing Place

Non-fiction

Healed and Souled

Don't Ask Me To Believe

Far From Home

Healing for Life

Finding Oasis

Survivor on Death Row *(co-written with Death Row inmate, Romell Broom)*

Website: https://clarenonhebel.com

Printed in Poland
by Amazon Fulfillment
Poland Sp. z o.o., Wrocław

49468350R00073